personal coaching

personal coaching

releasing potential at work

kaye thorne

KOGAN
PAGE

First published in 2001

Kogan Page Limited   Stylus Publishing Inc.
120 Pentonville Road   22883 Quicksilver Drive
London   Sterling
N1 9JN   VA 20166-2012
UK   USA

© Kaye Thorne, 2001

British Library Cataloguing in Publication Data

A CIP record for this book is available from the British Library.

ISBN 0 7494 3589 5

Typeset by D & N Publishing, Marlborough, Wiltshire
Printed and bound in Great Britain by Clays Ltd, St Ives plc

Dedication

To Andy Pellant.

James Redfield describes the Seventh Insight in *The Celestine Prophecy* as Engaging the Flow:

> Knowing our personal mission further enhances the flow of mysterious coincidences as we are guided towards our destinies. First we have a question, then dreams, daydreams and intuitions which lead us toward the answers which are usually synchronistically provided by the wisdom of another human being.

Andy, thank you for your humour, your insight and for touching my soul. You have taught me to be strong, to explore my emotions and through your wisdom to trust my intuition and to find my answers.

Contents

Contents

Contents

Foreword

My vision in writing this book is to combine the principles of best practice in coaching with the natural behaviours of sharing insights, storytelling and learning that have always existed in our communities. It is based on a desire to help create and support a culture of one-to-one development, enhanced feedback and a climate of high support.

Personal coaching is at the core of many powerful learning experiences. It encourages a learner to take significant steps in assimilating knowledge and developing new skills. It is also about setting people free and enabling them to revel in that new freedom.

This book is about helping people to fulfil their potential: it is about helping them to develop a full understanding of themselves through awakening their senses, gaining insight about who they really are and helping them to build personal resilience and strength through a greater understanding of themselves.

Personal coaching is like helping people to take a blank canvas, but as they start to work on their picture they realize that, in fact, it is not blank and that as they use their brush over the top of the canvas certain parts gain more focus and they recognize parts of the background, which they can choose to enhance or paint over if they so wish.

In acting as a personal coach you will be embarking on a journey with a learner that may be life changing. You will be forming a special relationship that should be nurtured, cherished and treated with great care. In helping them to soar you will need to help them overcome the fear of failing and to inspire their confidence and willingness to try and try again so that they can unlock their hidden potential. In the words of Mark Twain: 'One learns through the heart, not the eyes, or the intellect.'

Acknowledgements

Writing this book was a special experience for me. It was the opportunity to share some very personal thoughts and ideas about how to help people learn and develop. Taking the time to focus on our own development is something that we rarely do.

I would like, in these acknowledgements, to pay tribute to my family, friends, colleagues, clients and fellow authors who over the years have given me the inspiration, courage and support to explore my own learning and to push the boundaries of discovery.

First, my family: my father Kelvin Harris who, at 81, is a daily inspiration to me. My son Matt, whose creativity and personal commitment to excellence in his own writing is an inspiring example. My daughter Louise for her courage and energy in taking off across the world to work and live in Australia while still taking time to create and design the models in this book for me.

My close work colleagues, Steve Bedford and the whole team at Learn 2 Earn Ltd, Chris and Vivien Dunn and the whole team at TDA Transitions Ltd. You have always been there for me providing the vision, personal support, and inspiring me with different, interesting and stimulating projects.

My previous co-authors, Alex Machray and David Mackey, for your commitment, personal support and sharing of knowledge in our collaborations.

Mark Woodhouse for your personal support and always being an example of leading edge organizational development, and for constantly striving to achieve training excellence.

John Kenney for sharing your wisdom on personal coaching and always being willing to give valuable feedback.

Ian Anderson, retiring this year, in recognition of all the tremendous work that you have done in encouraging community investment.

Kevin McGrath, for all the quiet support you provide, your thoughtfulness and care.

Paul Ewins for all your wisdom and financial advice, which is critical to me as a small business.

Dr Alan Stanhope for your creativity and inspiration and providing such an excellent example of how to create a learning environment.

Ian Banyard, and Llorett Kemplen, two inspiring trainer colleagues who have done so much to support me and promote my work.

Keith Harriss and family, for always being there, on time, and a constant source of support.

Alan Smith for your care and humour, and acting as a sounding board.

Rob and Sue Ford and all the tmag team for providing me with an ongoing opportunity to exercise my creativity through writing articles.

Margaret and Les Ellyatt, Bill and Bernice Legg, Sidney and Elizabeth Cole, Eileen and Gordon Nicholls, Charles and Jean Burrows, Diana and Nigel Gray, William Henwood, Joy and Peter Gunson, thank you for your support, care and ongoing kindness.

The Kilby Family at The Garrack Hotel, St Ives, Cornwall for your personal support and providing the most inspiring place to write.

There are a number of other close friends and colleagues to whom I also owe a great debt of gratitude for their ongoing care, support and genuine interest. You are each very special but the only way I can give credit to you all is to list you alphabetically: Paul Allen, Rosemary Anderson, Keith Bastin, Richard and Lindy Bishop, Babs Bonner, Vivien Bolton, Richard Challinor, Margaret Cortis, Bill Eldridge, Caroline, Ross, Ben and Laura Garside, Chris George, Mark Gordon, Will and Anya Keith, Peter Lightfoot, Cheri Lofland, Chris Phelps, Sheila Rundle, Lesley Shaw, Doug and Lisa Twining, my trainer colleagues and all the very special clients and individual learners who ultimately have been my inspiration and without whom this book would never have been written — my particular thanks to you.

I also want to acknowledge the work of those who created the models and concepts that underpin many personal coaching activities and for whom I cannot find specific references: SMART, Unconscious Competence, Urgent/Important; numerous quotations from individuals that are acknowledged to the individual, but the original source is unknown; Tony Buzan for his innovative mind map method; Peter Honey and Alan Mumford for the Learning Styles Questionnaire; David A Kolb for the inspiration behind 'How People Learn' and his experiential learning model; Joseph Luft and Harry Ingham for the Johari Window, and all the staff at the CIPD and IoD Libraries for their help in compiling the bibliography.

There is a list of authors mentioned in the bibliography, but special thanks have to go to three authors. First, Daniel Goleman: *Working With Emotional Intelligence* is one of the most inspiring books that I have ever read. Second, Joe Jaworski: *Synchronicity: The Inner Path of Leadership* is a thoughtful examination of the concept of synchronicity. James Redfield and Carol Adrienne: *The Celestine Prophecy: The experiential guide*. If you want to start your own personal journey, there is no better place to begin than with this book. All three should be on the bookshelf of any personal coach.

Finally a very personal thanks to Philip Mudd at Kogan Page, who has been my editor for the last five years. You are a brilliant example of how to get the best from a writer, you give me freedom to write, you inspire me to come up with new ideas and you always come back promptly with valuable feedback.

My grateful thanks to you all.

Introduction

Success begins the moment we understand that life is about growing, it is about acquiring the knowledge and skills to live more fully and effectively. Life is meant to be a never-ending education and when this is fully appreciated we are no longer survivors, but adventurers. Life becomes a journey of discovery, an exploration into our potential. Any joy and exuberance we experience in living are the fruits of our willingness to risk, our openness to change and our ability to create what we want for our lives.

(David McNally, *Even Eagles Need a Push*)

This book is about personal coaching, which is a special one-to-one relationship built to support individuals as they make choices about their life and work. In the same way that a personal trainer would work with you to tone your body, personal coaching works with your mind and spirit. When it is done well the connectivity is seamless – your coach intuitively knows how and when to suggest meetings at times that will uplift you.

Personal coaches encourage you to step outside your day-to-day routine – they help you to explore the boundaries of your learning and support and challenge you at times of decision. They can be sounding boards, mentors and friends. They can stimulate, excite and encourage you to step outside your comfort zone and, because the relationship is built on professionalism, integrity and trust, you will push yourself that little harder to achieve your goals. Like athletes with their trainers, you plan a training regime together, you agree the times when you want to be challenged to test your resistance and personal strength of mind, but equally they encourage you to wind down after you have put yourself through a challenging situation.

They help you to visualize your success and to surround yourself with images and stimuli to fuel your imagination and to help you to recharge. They weave in and out of your life, helping you to create a tapestry of experiences that help you to grow and develop.

So could you be a personal coach? This book is written for anyone who wants to offer personal coaching. You might be any one of the following:

- a member of a training-and-development, or human resources function;
- a line manager with responsibility for on-job coaching;
- an external training consultant;
- a lecturer in further or higher education;
- a senior executive who wishes to work on a one-to-one basis with the team.

Your job role might be trainer, performance coach, facilitator, developer, internal consultant or learning designer. Whatever your title, your interest will be in developing a skill set and creating an environment that is conducive to working with another person on a one-to-one basis.

ONLY THE FIRST STEP

It is important that this book should be read in the context of supporting personal development for coaches. A book should never be a substitute for the process of developing the skills required in becoming a coach. There are many professional qualifications available for coaches and if you are offering coaching it will be important to identify your own mentor who can help you to develop your skill set as a coach.

There are also a number of references throughout this book to the need to refer your participants to others for additional support. There are important differences between coaching and counselling and there may be times when you may recognize the need for specialist support. It is important that you not only recognize the need but that you help your participant to seek that additional help.

WHAT IS PERSONAL COACHING?

Personal coaching could be described as enabling – supporting another individual to achieve their personal goals. Within this context it uses a skill set that is similar to mentoring, or counselling. To coach someone successfully, it is likely that you will work within a coaching model of 'support and challenge' and will draw on the following skills: questioning, listening, observing and giving feedback. Although this mode of coaching is often used by senior executives the approach is relevant to anyone. The difference between personal coaching and coaching is that the coaching offered, like that provided by a personal sports trainer, very much focuses on the needs of the individual. It is driven by the individual and often looks holistically at their needs rather than being purely work related. You may also hear the term 'performance coach' and, although you may be helping someone improve their performance, personal coaching may not always be targeted at improving performance in a working environment. It may also be about encouraging learners to be more reflective and to focus on their behaviours rather than their competency development.

Often a plan is worked out between the coach and the participant that sets personal goals and targets and enables the participant to prepare for and take control of challenging situations. It is often very proactive and the relationship is built up over a period of time, which enables the coach to really develop a support-and-challenge approach.

ROLE OF THE PERSONAL COACH

Being a personal coach is like accompanying someone on a journey. It might be more accurate to describe a personal coach as a 'personal guide'. As in any journey it is important to prepare, to have an overall

3

sense of direction and then to build in special stepping stones. In acting as a guide there is the need to recognize that at certain times the individual will want 'guidance' and at other times will be ready to enjoy a process of self-discovery. As coaches we have a responsibility to grow close to our learners and to help them to know themselves.

By understanding how people learn and by building that knowledge in those that we coach we are actively demonstrating the saying 'give a man a rod and teach him to fish'.

HOW TO USE THIS BOOK

This book builds on the key concepts and ideas about training already discussed in previous companion books, *Everything You Ever Needed to Know About Training*, *Training on a Shoestring* and *World Class Training*. It will not train you to be a personal coach. It will give some insights into the role, highlight some of the skills that you will need, and suggest ways in which you may help your learner to learn. If you are serious about becoming a personal coach I hope it will encourage you to take the first step towards finding out more and to begin to build your own competencies as a coach. I hope that it will also encourage you to seek someone who could act as a personal coach to you and that it will encourage you to use self-coaching techniques to fulfil your hopes dreams and aspirations.

I hope you find it helpful in your own journey of self-discovery.

1

The role of a
personal coach

FINDING YOUR OWN PATH TO THE FUTURE

This chapter focuses on you as the coach. Your ability to support others needs to be matched by your ability to create your own development programme. By charting your own path to the future you create a very tangible way to empathize with the development needs of the individuals that you work with. Identifying personal goals and setting milestone plans for yourself will give you an intrinsic understanding of the issues and challenges faced by others. This is not to oversimplify the process, but much of the personal coaching process is based on a common sense approach to setting goals and planning routes to achieve them.

HOW PEOPLE LEARN

One of the most important aspects of personal coaching is recognizing the different needs of individual learners. This may have a real impact not only on *how* you coach but on *whom* you coach. Teachers, lecturers, trainers and workplace coaches may feel they have less choice in whom they work with, and there will be those who argue that coaching is a technique that, once learnt, can be applied with any combination of learners.

However, if you recall the people who have really influenced your learning it is very likely that there were very strong linkages between the way they taught you and the way that you wanted to learn. If we further develop this into the context of personal coaching it is even more likely that an effective coaching relationship is built on something other than just the pure techniques of coaching. One of the most important places to start is to develop as full as possible an understanding of how people learn and to recognize the key influences and research in this area.

One of the most enduring models about learning is Kolb's learning cycle. He identified key steps in how people learn and defined them as follows:

Having an experience

Having an experience, whether it is:

- managing a project;
- giving a presentation;
- completing a development activity;
- searching out new and challenging experiences, problems and opportunities;
- finding like-minded people to learn with;
- making mistakes;
- having fun.

Reflecting on the experience

In this context the personal coach can explore with individuals real experiences and situations that have helped to give them their world-views. Many coaching exercises and activities are built around this and encourage individuals to anchor and record what they know – for example:

- mapping your work/life history or your work experiences;
- reviewing the experiences and reflecting on what went well and what could have been improved, as well as seeking feedback from others;
- standing back from events to watch, listen and think;
- listening to a wide cross section of people with varying views;
- investigating by probing, assembling and analysing information;
- reviewing what has happened and what you have learnt.

Having worked through such exercises the personal coach will normally encourage the learner to reflect on those experiences and to identify what has been learnt. What is important at this stage is to encourage real and genuine reflection and this is where the coaching process can really help. Many self-help books encourage the learner to go through a process of recording and analysing. This is valuable but a coach can encourage a learner to reflect more on the experience by asking appropriate questions and knowing when to probe more deeply. Coaches can sense when it is important to encourage the learner to move on and when to lift the learner if they sense that perhaps the learner is dwelling too much on a particular area.

The power of personal exercises should never be underestimated and, for some individuals, activities such as completing a lifeline might highlight some painful experiences. As part of the initial contracting, it is important to spend time with learners, encouraging them to talk about their lives and careers, and noting down key experiences before you make an assessment of the right process.

Again this relates to your skill and experience as a coach. In any circumstances it is useful to know how your learners learn, their successes, and the areas where they have been less successful. However, it is even more important to help them believe in their success in the future. The power in reflective observation is the ability to rethink what has occurred.

One very useful technique that a coach can help a learner develop is *paradigm shift* (see Chapter 2). It could also be described as positive affirmation. It involves helping learners to shift their perspectives. The reason why this technique is important is that many of us are guilty of feeding our minds with negative thoughts. By developing the discipline of paradigm shift we re-educate our minds to go into situations and interpret them in a more positive light. The ease with which you and your learners will achieve this will also depend on your own perspective.

These first two stages can be quite lengthy and you may wish to work with your learners on key aspects of their experiences rather than trying to work across all areas. You can apply the Kolb model to a number of circumstances and in a cyclical way. You and your learner might prefer to focus on individual situations and work through them sequentially rather than handling everything at one go. In this way you are more likely to achieve completeness through a coaching session, rather than sending a learner away having opened up a number of areas but having been unable to process them effectively.

Theorizing about what happened

The next stage involves theorizing about what happened and why, then exploring options and alternatives. It involves:

- questioning and probing logic and assumptions;
- exploring ideas, concepts, theories, systems and models;
- exploring interrelationships between ideas, events and situations;
- formulating your own theories or models.

This stage is where the coach and the learner work to create a new way of doing things into the reality of their current lives and develop an implementation plan. This process is cyclical so that a learner who has absorbed one set of learning experiences is ready to undertake the process again with another learning experience.

Planning what to do differently next time

This involves:

- finding out how the experts do it;
- looking for practical applications of ideas;
- finding opportunities to implement or teach what you learn;
- trying out and practising techniques with coaching and feedback.

The first time that many individuals experience coaching in the work-place is in a remedial situation, yet one of the most powerful stages in the learning process is active experimentation. When we first learn as children it is the experimentation that is so enjoyable. As adults we should also be able to indulge in this, too. So much of adult life is geared around 'think it and do it'. Far less time is spent on exploration. Explorers are sometimes criticized as people who unnecessarily hold up a process and yet the wisdom generated by taking time to explore, or to revisit a subject and provide a different perspective, can be invaluable.

It is important to recognize that not all learning may take place in a neat and ordered way. We learn best when we combine the following four approaches to learning:

- theory input;

- practical experience;

- application of theory;

- idea generation.

Kolb's learning cycle is also linked to work of Honey and Mumford and their learning styles questionnaire.

We all prefer to learn in slightly different ways:

- activists learn best by doing;

- reflectors learn best by observing;

- theorists learn best by thinking things through in a logical and systematic manner;

- pragmatists like to learn through putting their ideas into practice and testing them out.

To find out more about you or your learner's preferred learning style you may wish to undertake the Honey and Mumford Learning Styles

Questionnaire (contact Peter Honey at www.peterhoney.com). The definitions below give you some examples of the different types of learning style. Try to identify which of the learning styles appeals to you.

Activists

- Enjoy new experiences and opportunities from which they can learn.

- Often do things first and think about them later.

- Enjoy being involved: are happy to be in the limelight and prefer to be active rather than sitting and listening.

- Often look for new challenges.

- Like to learn with people who are like-minded.

- Are willing to make mistakes.

- Like to have fun when they are learning.

Reflectors

- Prefer to stand back from events, to watch and absorb information before starting.

- Like to hear other people's viewpoints.

- Like to review what has happened, and what they have learned.

- Prefer to reach decisions in their own time.

- Do not like to feel under pressure.

Theorists

- Like to explore methodically, to think problems through in a step-by-step logical way and ask questions.

- Can be detached and analytical.

■ Like to be intellectually stretched and may feel uncomfortable with lateral thinking, preferring models and systems.

■ Prefer to come up with their own theories or models.

Pragmatists

■ Like practical solutions and want to get on and try things.

■ Dislike too much theory.

■ Sometimes like to find out how the experts do it.

■ Like to experiment and search out new ideas that they want to try out.

■ Tend to act quickly and confidently.

■ Very down-to-earth and respond to problems as challenges.

You may find that you have a preference for one or two learning styles or that, like a small percentage of people, you have a balanced learning style. Kolb's ideas about learning and Honey and Mumford's learning styles link well together. They also link with the following model of how people learn something new.

UNCONSCIOUS INCOMPETENCE
I don't know what I don't know and I don't know that I don't know it. Ignorance is bliss!

CONSCIOUS INCOMPETENCE
I know there are things that I should know, but I am not able to do them yet.

CONSCIOUS COMPETENCE
I know what I should know and how to use my knowledge to put it effectively into practice.

UNCONSCIOUS COMPETENCE
I now do things without consciously thinking about how I do it.

USING THE WHOLE BRAIN

As well as understanding your learning style you will also have a preferred way of operating using the left or right part of your brain. The research of Sperry and Onstein points out that we have two hemispheres in our brain, which have different characteristics or specializations:

LEFT BRAIN	RIGHT BRAIN
Logic	Rhythm
Lists	Colour
Linear	Imagination
Words	Day dreaming
Numbers	Intuition
Sequence	Spatial awareness
Analysis	Music

If one side of your brain has always dominated you might find it harder to use the skills associated with the other. You might believe that you are no good at a particular subject – for example, you might say 'I am no good at maths', or 'I've never been able to draw'. However, researchers like Tony Buzan who developed the Mind Maps® technique are showing that we need not be totally left-brained or right-brained, but that by using both sides of our brain in our activities become more 'whole-brained'.

Once you understand your preferences, and the more you understand about how you learn, you can use this knowledge to accelerate your learning and to make your learning experiences more meaningful.

INTELLIGENCES

If you are really interested in finding out more about how people learn you might be interested in the work of Howard Gardner, a prominent psychologist who argues that everybody possesses at least seven intelligences. Find out more by reading Gardner's *Frames of Mind* (1993).

The following list is based on and adapted from research by Howard Gardner. Use the list to work through with your learners the best way for them to learn.

- *Linguistic intelligence.* The intelligence of words. People with high linguistic intelligence like to read, write and are good at spelling, verbal and written communication. They like learning from books, tapes, lectures and presentations.

- *Logical–mathematical intelligence.* The intelligence of logic and numbers. People with high logical-mathematical intelligence like experimenting with things in an orderly and controlled manner. They learn by creating and solving problems, and by playing mathematical games.

- *Musical intelligence.* The intelligence of rhythm, music and lyrics. They may play musical instruments, often sing or hum to themselves, and like relaxing to music. They learn by using music and may use rhymes to help remember.

- *Spatial intelligence.* The intelligence of mental pictures and images. They normally think and remember in pictures, and like drawing, painting and sculpting. They may use symbols, doodles, diagrams and mind maps to learn.

- *Bodily/kinesthetic intelligence.* The intelligence of expression through physical activities. They are often good with their hands. They like physical activity, sports, games, drama, dancing and learn through doing, taking action, writing notes. Need frequent breaks when learning.

- *Interpersonal intelligence.* The intelligence of communicating with others. They know how to organize, relate and tune into others and to put people at ease. They learn from others, they like learning in teams, comparing notes, socializing and teaching.

- *Intrapersonal intelligence.* The intelligence of self-discovery. They often prefer to work alone and like peace and quiet. They often daydream, are intuitive, they keep a diary, plan their time carefully, and are independent. They learn by setting personal goals, taking control of their learning, reflecting on their experiences.

Howard's work is also linked to Daniel Goleman's work on 'emotional intelligence' (see Chapter 2) and Honey and Mumford's 'learning styles' (see page 12).

If your learners enjoy the learning experience they are more likely to learn and remember. If they are *told* that they need to learn something, their willingness to learn will depend on the respect that they have for the person telling them and their desire to learn.

If their desire to learn is driven by a personal curiosity and they learn in a way that reflects their preferred learning style it is likely that their own enthusiasm and interest will make the learning more meaningful and memorable.

Apply the following to your own learning and ask your learner to consider the following questions:

- Have I created the right place for me to learn?

- Do I take responsibility for my learning?

- Do I use my preferred learning styles?

- Can I learn despite poor teaching?

- Do I seek additional coaching?

- Am I actively involved in the learning process?

- Can I learn in many different ways?

- Do I know what I need to memorize, what I need to understand and what I need to 'learn by doing'?

- Do I seek feedback on my learning, on my performance?

- Do I learn from my mistakes?

- Do I regularly take a break and do something else to energize myself?

- Do I share and celebrate my successes in learning?

REFLECTING ON LEARNING

An important part of your learning is to help your learners to review the outcomes of their development activities. Encourage them to ask themselves the following after a learning event:

- What went well? Why?

- What could have gone better? Why?

- How could I improve next time?

- What have I learned?

- How will I use this learning in the future?

HELPING YOURSELF TO HELP OTHERS

There are so many ways in which you can develop your own skills to enable you to help others. The very nature of personal coaching is based on the traditional ways that people have always learnt. There are the underpinning skills of effective communication, observing, questioning, listening and giving feedback, but there is also a range of other techniques and ways in which you can help individuals to explore their own development.

As you grow in knowledge you can help a learner to take the steps along their road to fulfilling their potential. Some of the important influences worth considering are neuro-linguistic programming (NLP) and emotional intelligence. These and other techniques and influences like storytelling and synchronicity are also explored in Chapter 2 and Chapter 5.

IDENTIFYING YOUR OWN STYLE

Always recognize where your learner is starting from. Although you may develop a richer and deeper understanding of how people learn and of personal motivation, and although you may explore new philosophies and alternative ways of working, assimilate this knowledge, use it to heighten your own understanding, but never use your learner as a guinea-pig to test your half-formed theories. A little knowledge can be a dangerous thing and any reputable theory of development should have either an accreditation or a practitioner development programme. Reading about something can only ever be a first step; to develop full understanding you need to follow the steps in Kolb's learning cycle.

INVITING FEEDBACK

Who gives you feedback? Do you invite it? Do you believe it? As professionals, we should be able to ask for and absorb feedback into our ongoing development. Unfortunately there are very few people who are really skilled at giving it. If you are training people to assess or coach, you will recognize the importance of doing it properly. It is one area that consistently causes issues in organizations, so many people give feedback that is unhelpful during appraisals or performance management sessions. With less opportunity for training, there are ever more instances of unskilled feedback.

If you do develop a clear understanding of your strengths, you are better able to help people give you feedback. By asking the right questions you will be able to elicit information about your own performance. If you develop experience as a communicator, you will also be able to identify other people's responses to you. There will be several references to giving effective feedback in this book but as a personal coach you really do need to consider feedback in a number of contexts:

■ How effective am I at giving feedback? How do I know? How could I check my understanding?

■ Do I ask for feedback? If yes, with what result? If no, what positive actions can I take to overcome this?

■ Who do I really trust to help me explore the areas where I feel less confident?

■ How can I enhance my skills in giving feedback?

■ What would I like to do differently when giving feedback?

The above list of questions is intended to provide prompts for you to consider, but as part of your personal development you might want to explore these in more depth with your own personal coach, or mentor.

SELECTING YOUR OWN PERSONAL COACH

A personal coach is more than someone who you can turn to for help or advice. This person is different from your parents, partner, lover, or best friend. This is someone who endures over time, who will listen to your ideas, will help you talk through your deepest concerns and ultimately allow you to make up your own mind. What personal coaches really do is to provide a sounding board. You respect them for their views and they are a great source of inspiration. The nature of the relationship ought to be formalized, and there should be an agreement between you that so that you are both aware of your responsibilities. This will apply equally when you are offering personal coaching to others. They and you, when you are acting in the role of a personal coach, should adhere to a code of practice. There should be a duty of care so that everyone recognizes the full level of responsibility and acts accordingly.

Think carefully about who you choose as a personal coach, particularly if you are offering personal coaching to others. Do not simply make an informal arrangement with a colleague because you know each other and you get on well. If you are serious about your personal growth you need to identify someone who will stretch you and help you to develop new skills. The more experienced you are the longer it may take to find the right person. To help you in your choice you may want to consider the following checklist:

- Do you trust them?

- Do you respect their opinion?

- Do they have the time to meet with you?

- How have they developed their expertise? Are they actively developing their own potential?

- Can you relax with them?

- Could they help you to set 'SMART' (Specific, Measurable, Achievable, Realistic, Timed) and 'stretch' goals (see below)?

- Could they help you to develop new skills and knowledge?

- Could they inspire you to keep going when the going gets tough?

- Could they help you to grow your network?

- Would your life be less enriched without them?

The best coaches also fill you with enthusiasm. You feel better for spending time with them or talking on the telephone to them. We often identify them over a period of time. What distinguishes them from our friends, family or colleagues is their wisdom and our respect for them. We feel comfortable with them. We accept the challenges that they set us and we want them to be proud of us.

COULD YOU BE A PERSONAL COACH?

As discussed in the foreword and introduction to this book, the role of a personal coach has evolved from the principles of a variety of forms of coaching. What is really important is not attempting to work as a personal coach without developing competence. It is equally important to recognize the boundaries. In the context of personal coaching within this book, the role of a personal coach is about developing the competence to help people help themselves. It is about skilfully using observation, questioning, listening and giving feedback to enable learners to take their own journey of discovery. The emphasis should always be on what they are going to do to take ownership of their journey and your role will be one of a personal guide and sounding board, helping them to explore options and choices.

The difference with personal coaching is that it is personal, and as such it should focus completely on the individual learner. You can help learners to understand how they relate to others and, importantly, why that interconnectivity works better with some people rather than others. By enabling learners to discover their uniqueness you can also help them to enjoy and reflect on the synergy of their relationships with others. (See Figure 1.1 on page 23)

RECOGNIZING YOUR OWN BOUNDARIES

As a personal coach it is important that you should recognize a number of boundaries. The first boundary is about encouraging learners to take responsibility for their own decisions. This rule above all others is a fundamental point that not only reflects your own professionalism, but is also critical for the individual. Although you may work very closely with individual learners you must never make their decisions for them.

Another important boundary is often mentioned – the difference between coaching and counselling. You may, in your work, reach a point where individuals are in need of counselling support. Always help them to seek this specialist help. Do not attempt to offer counselling support. Even if you are a trained counsellor you also need to recognize how the nature of your coaching relationship may change if you also offer counselling support to the same learner.

DEVELOPING NEW SKILLS

Everyone who is helping others to learn needs to be aware of the need to keep developing their own skills. Chapter 5 will help you to identify key areas that you might wish to develop but in each chapter of this book there might be other areas that you wish to explore further.

Setting your own development plan

One of the critical learning points for individuals is the realization that they in fact are in control of their own destiny. In helping someone on their own particular journey it is so important that learners recognize and understand the process and acknowledge insights as they occur for them. This is another important function of coaches: they can help to raise the awareness of the stages in undertaking personal discovery not just for their learners but also for themselves.

I am able to build rapport with a range of learners	1	2	3	4
I show genuine interest in people	1	2	3	4
I have underpinning knowledge about psychometrics/profiling	1	2	3	4
I am accredited to give feedback about psychometrics/profiling	1	2	3	4
I am able to give effective feedback	1	2	3	4
I am able to ask the full range of coaching questions	1	2	3	4
I am have a high level of listening skills	1	2	3	4
I am able to implement all stages of the coaching process	1	2	3	4
I have a good understanding of the impact of personal coaching	1	2	3	4
I maintain an effective personal and professional network	1	2	3	4
I have a well developed range of coping strategies	1	2	3	4
I have an implementation plan for my own personal development	1	2	3	4

1. Need more skill/knowledge
2. Need more practice
3. Competent
4. Consistently competent

Use this form to identify improvement areas that you would like to focus on.

Figure 1.1 Personal coaching self-assessment questionnaire

2

Recognizing the
needs of the
individual

CREATING A CLIMATE OF TRUST

One of the most important parts of being a personal coach is establishing trust. Without this nothing can really start. In this context, establishing trust involves confirming to the learner that everything that is said between the two of you is completely confidential. It also means creating a sense of care, empathy and total professionalism. This is the foundation of the whole relationship. It means reassuring learners that their thoughts, hopes, dreams and aspirations are safe with you. It means that, through your actions and the way that you conduct the relationship, they feel confident in your ability to work with them and support them. It also means that you keep your own concerns, worries and views to yourself and don't use the sessions for your own gain.

It is also important to recognize that trust, once betrayed, is highly unlikely ever to be regained, and that you therefore do everything in your power to maintain it. Never *ever* repeat anything that is said to you in a coaching session to anyone else, however professional or trustworthy you believe that person to be. Once it has been shared you no longer have any control over how it is shared or repeated and you have broken the confidence of the learner who trusted you.

The implications of this are highlighted when you find yourself in a situation when you feel unable to offer the right support to your learner. What do you do? It is important that you gain agreement about what to do next. The options may be to encourage your learner to seek additional help or to gain agreement that on a specific issue you will seek advice from someone else on the learner's behalf. The latter can only be undertaken with their express permission and with agreement on the elements of disclosure.

In many ways it is preferable to work with learners to enable them to seek support themselves. That way they retain ownership of the issue and they also know what information has been shared. This has particular relevance in workplace coaching where the coach may not be the line manager but learners may raise issues about their relationship with their managers. In this context it is always preferable to support individuals as they work through the issue, but to encourage them to work with their manager to resolve the issue.

There might be occasions when you feel that your learners may need specialist help. This might be related to technical matters or skills, it might involve a need for additional training, or it might be a need for counselling to help them work through a particular issue. It is very important that you handle this up front at the start of the relationship by clearly explaining your role, skills and expertise and how you would work with your learners to prepare them to work with others, but do not try to offer counselling within your role as a coach. The underpinning skill set may be similar, but counselling is a very specialist area, and only people properly trained and qualified in this area should offer counselling support.

EVERYONE IS DIFFERENT

Everyone *is* different and it is essential to gain an understanding of the differences if you are to work as a personal coach with anyone. This understanding is based on a number of key factors.

Each individual learner that you coach will be different, and you will be different to them. Recognizing these differences is an important part of coaching and helping others to learn. What is fascinating is recognizing how subtle these differences are. No two people will have exactly the same combination, and in this context we should never make broad assumptions about different learners.

One way that you can help individuals to gain personal insight is by encouraging them to build an understanding of themselves. One phrase that sums this up is 'being comfortable with yourself'. This phrase is used to describe that inner confidence that comes from knowing your strengths and areas of development. With this inner confidence also comes an ability to accept challenges and to want to explore your personal boundaries and comfort zones. Without this understanding there is a danger that the learner may not be able to respond positively to feedback from others.

We can build a picture of ourselves through a variety of means, but the model in Figure 2.1, which is adapted from the original model found in *Everything You Ever Needed to Know about Training* (Thorne and

Mackey, 2001), illustrates the type of analysis that we can undertake to gain a clearer picture of ourselves, and even more importantly, how others perceive us.

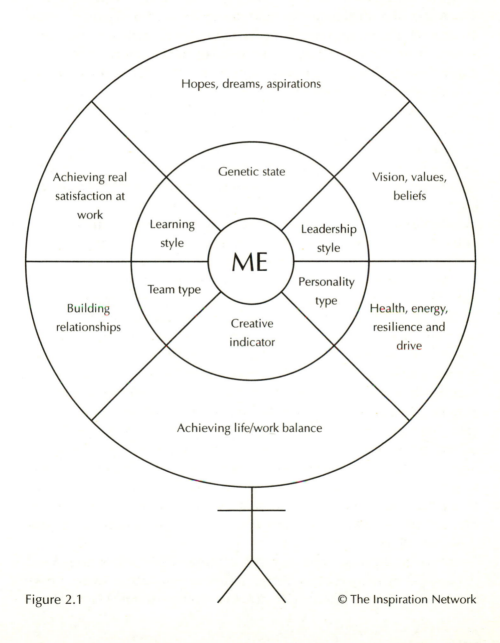

Figure 2.1

© The Inspiration Network

As a personal coach in the workplace you may initially find it easier to talk through the inner ring; however, behind the inner ring are a number of more personal areas such as health, relationships, work/life balance, finances.

Traditionally discussion around these areas has normally only occurred at the point when someone is being made redundant and a redundancy counsellor may have encouraged an exiting employee to think about the implications of being made redundant, on their family, their lifestyle and their finances.

Health was often only addressed if the individual became ill, often as the result of a more serious 'wake-up' call and, although organizations may run stress-management programmes for employees, comparatively few address it proactively or offer tangible help to enable employees to deal with the underlying causes. However, if you are going to offer support in the role of a personal coach all these additional areas are really important in helping the individuals take charge of their lives and work to make a difference.

When working with learners we can build on this picture by probing deeper into particular areas – encouraging them to undertake reputable psychometric tests or to use personal profiling tools. We can also help them to make linkages between the outcomes, exploring with them the implications of this information for the way that they achieve their personal goals, or the impact of this in the way that they work with others. It is important to help learners to realize that these models of them are not static and that lifetime learning will help them to develop new layers of knowledge and understanding.

Repeating some of the profiling later may reveal new insights about how they have developed. As we mature we change, and so our responses will change. Some characteristics may remain the same but as individuals become more experienced and more at ease with the ongoing process of self-development they will gain a new richness of understanding.

As a personal coach you may find it valuable to become accredited to administer and give feedback on a number of profiling tools, or psychometric tests. Not only will this give you personal insight about yourself but you will be able to work with your learner to develop their understanding.

As mentioned in Chapter 1, developing your own skill set is an important part of being a personal coach, but without developing this understanding it will be very difficult to help your learners chart their journey.

CLIENT CONFIDENTIALITY

If you are acting as a personal coach within an organization you need to recognize the significance of your role. Where organizations have offered counselling support it tends to be supplied by an outside agency. Personal coaches have some of the same issues: confidentiality, trust, relationships with line managers, loyalty to the organization. Like the role of the internal consultant, these interrelationships need to be worked out first so that everyone is absolutely clear about the roles, responsibilities and boundaries.

ANALYSING DEVELOPMENT NEEDS

In working with people it is important that you help them to recognize that who they are will impact on what they want to do and how they are able to achieve their goals.

By undertaking psychometric tests or profiling you will help them gain insight into who they are, but by encouraging them to recognize the impact and importance of the outer ring you will enable them to view their own development in the context of the bigger picture.

One important point to emphasize here is that one of the roles of a personal coach is to help the individual to develop self-motivation. There are many motivational books, videos, cassettes and speakers that can help to stimulate an individual to become more motivated but, in the same way that New Year's resolutions fail, the individual will only sustain real change if they continue to work at it. This is where a personal coach can really add value.

Some of the major roles of a personal coach include helping individuals to recognize the reality of how they handle change, encouraging them to recognize the steps needed to sustain change, and regularly helping them to energize so that they can continue on their journey. . Just as a personal trainer will build in maintenance exercises, you need to encourage your learners to do the same. It is equally important to encourage learners to regularly undertake a review of what they have achieved. This is much easier if they have set SMART goals (see Chapters 3 and 5) so that they have time lines to review progress against.

Within the context of the model it is important to recognize that this is only the top level of an underpinning skill, knowledge and competence set, and once the key areas are analysed, then you can work with the learner to identify key areas of development.

THE INNER CIRCLE

This circle (see Figure 2.2 on page 38) is created to illustrate some of the areas where psychometric and profiling tests have been developed to measure preferences and the underpinning personality and characteristics of an individual learner. What is important is not necessarily the specific areas highlighted but to identify a range of tools that will serve to give the individual feedback which helps them to identify who they are. It is important to help the learner to recognize that this can only be a snapshot in time. This knowledge is enhanced and developed through feedback.

EMOTIONAL INTELLIGENCE

Individuals and organizations are increasingly recognizing the richness that can also be considered by examining more personal areas such as the emotional competence framework identified by Daniel Goleman in his book *Working with Emotional Intelligence*.

Although it might seem that 'emotional intelligence' is a recent entrant into our vocabulary it has, in fact, been acknowledged for a much longer period. Goleman suggests that a number of people have defined emotional intelligence including Howard Gardner, who in 1983 proposed a model of 'multiple intelligence', and Peter Salovey and John Mayer in the 1990s who defined emotional intelligence 'in terms of being able to monitor and regulate one's own and others' feelings and to use feelings to guide thought and action.'

Goleman's own definition includes five basic emotional and social competencies:

- self-awareness;
- self-regulation;
- motivation;
- empathy;
- social skills.

Goleman's work moves emotional intelligence into the arena of emotional competence by further defining 25 emotional competencies and explaining that individuals will have a profile of strengths and limits but that 'the ingredients for outstanding performance require only that we have strengths in a given number of these competencies, typically at least six or so, and that the strengths be spread across all five areas of emotional intelligence. In other words there are many paths to excellence.'

What Goleman and others have done is to introduce the concept of another type of intelligence and to suggest that our skills with people are as important to the organizations that might recruit us as our IQ, our qualifications and our expertise. Many organizations are also recognizing the impact of this in their retention and development of key workers. These personal competencies, together with other traits and characteristics, are an integral part of the picture that you will develop with your learner. As the two of you look at the blank canvas you will begin to be able to start painting in parts of the background and to a certain extent some of the foreground based on the knowledge of what is intrinsic and important to the individual.

This is still a comparatively new area for individuals – particularly in some corporate environments where any assessment tends to be more about performance rather than helping individuals discover more about themselves. You may also encounter resistance from some individuals and this is primarily because they do not see the value of such feedback. This may be because of previous experiences, or because no one has taken the time to explain to them the value of tests/profiles.

In personal coaching we need to get underneath any system of classification and focus in much more detail on individuals and their uniqueness. The top-line results can be a useful starting point but we need to spend time helping individuals gain a more holistic view of themselves and to use that initial understanding as a basic template on which to build. It can also help to use this information to compare and contrast results and to identify similarities and complementary preferences.

Therefore, as a starting point in your coaching sessions, ask individuals to bring the results of these inventories, preference tools and psychometric tests. Spend time asking them to identify the highlights and questions from them about their results. Try to identify similar responses, outcomes and results. Ask probing questions to help learners own and recognize what is important for them in the way that they learn or interact with others. Use these results as a basis for establishing how the two of you should work together. Help them to identify how they can build on their preferences in the way that they learn or develop new skills.

Encourage them to see each part of their profile as a building block in the foundations of their development. Help them to recognize that the better they know themselves the better able they will be to develop new skills and insights in the future. Without this inner self-awareness it would be like building a home with no foundations: there is always the danger that it will collapse. However, the deeper and more secure the foundations, the more stable will be the house. Remember that, in areas prone to earthquakes, the buildings have special flexibility built in that allows them to withstand some tremors. The analogy is useful to remember because when working with individuals we often need inbuilt resilience and flexibility to help us cope with some situations.

JOHARI'S WINDOW

Essentially what this process does is help the individual explore the broader issues of what they want to achieve. There are many tools and techniques that you can use to support a learner through personal coaching (see Chapter 5) but, in the context of this model, Johari's window can be particularly valuable.

The Johari window, named after its creators Joseph Luft and Harry Ingham, helps individuals to gain insight into how they operate and how open they are to others.

The *open* pane of the window represents those things in their life that they know about and that you know about. Things that are clearly visible like gender, height, or other messages that they intentionally convey to people. The openness of this may vary from individual to individual but essentially this is the public image.

The *hidden* pane of the window is what the learner is less willing to share. These are the private hopes, dreams and aspirations. They may also be things that have happened in the past that they do not want others to know about.

The *blind* pane of the window concerns things that other people know about the individual, but the individual does not know them. This is where feedback from others can help the individual discover more about themselves.

The *unknown* pane of the window is that which is hidden from the individual and also from others. It could be the individual's future potential, or the way that they may react under certain circumstances because they had not experienced those circumstances before.

Helping individuals to gain greater insight through giving them appropriate feedback and helping them to explore the areas that they don't normally share is one of the fundamental points behind personal coaching but, as emphasized throughout this book, it has to be given at an appropriate time and in an appropriate place. Creating the right level of trust, allowing the necessary amount of time and not over-whelming the learner with multiple questions are all important in helping the individual undertake meaningful change.

THE OUTER CIRCLE

The areas identified here show you how you could encourage learners to review some of the key aspects of their personal development. Use of the Johari window model has to be negotiated with learners. They might be interested in seeing the overall model, but they might say that their current main interests are in the skills, knowledge and compe-tencies segment. Your judgement will be the point at which to intro-duce a model of the bigger picture and to work with them to enable them to set their own learning agenda.

Also try to find a time and create an environment that is more con-ducive to creative thought. This may be more appropriate off site. When working through this session help learners to refine their hopes by asking clarifying questions, particularly if you can help learners to identify time frames.

Under each of these groups of questions there are a series of sub-questions followed by a means of building up the skills and compe-tencies into a development plan. Some areas are more personal than others. It might not be appropriate to discuss an individual's finances, or the long-term care solution for an aged relative, or a deep issue in a personal relationship. It is important that you enable your learner to recognize that these areas are factors that they have to consider and that if they put time aside to address the issues this will help them in other aspects of their life.

Sometimes when individuals survey their wheels of life they feel quite daunted by the total picture. Again this is where you can offer support. Show them how, by using different techniques like 'GROW', or 'SMART' (see Chapter 5) they can start to take incremental steps towards a solution. You can also help them to identify external sources of support such as financial advisers, advice centres or other sources of professional support.

At the end of each section below are some examples of questions that you might ask, as ever these are only examples. The list is not exhaustive. What it does is to start the process of encouraging the learner to undertake a sense check. It is the first step towards helping them to explore each area and the impact of each area on the other.

Special note: you need to create your own list that is appropriate for your learners, their particular set of circumstances and the style in which you work with them.

What you are working towards is achieving a sense of balance, helping them to achieve a greater understanding of their core, their personal profile and their preferences. They will then be able to focus on the outer circle with heightened insight and be better able to relate and communicate with others. With this increased self-awareness comes the need for learners to take time out regularly to focus on themselves. Initially this may prove to be difficult; in today's busy environment very few people get the opportunity to take time out to think, reflect or indulge themselves by doing something that they really want to do. Suggesting that they start by taking 20 minutes each day for themselves and working up to an hour may be a challenge. For people who are naturally anxious and spend their time rushing around, stopping and sitting still may be an unknown concept.

As an example, here are some of the questions and areas for consideration.

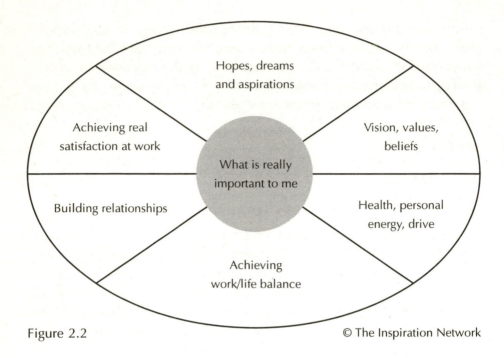

Figure 2.2 © The Inspiration Network

Hopes, dreams and aspirations

By asking open questions you can help the individual begin to identify areas that they wish to work on. Remember that, if they are unused to setting goals, seeing different alternatives will take time. Asking an open question such as 'What would you like to do in the future?' to an adult can be as threatening as asking a young person 'What do you want to do when you leave school?' They simply may not know. However helping people to start to identify their goals is important. Encouraging individuals to give themselves permission to dream is a valuable part of the role of being a personal coach.

At this stage what you want to achieve are the more long-term bigger picture goals and in some cases fantasies. It is also important that they don't shut down opportunities – for example 'I would love to get promoted, but I know I won't.' Some learners will naturally build a denial or negative statement onto the back of their hopes dreams and aspirations. Work with them to articulate only the positive statements and to log these thoughts, which can be translated later into SMART goals. At this stage it is important to help them to keep the thoughts flowing rather than stop the process to write the right words. It will also help the learner if you have outlined the key areas before so that they can start thinking prior to the session.

Possible questions

Do you have an overall sense of direction?

Can you articulate your aspirations?

Do you actively pursue your dreams, or do you see them as pure fantasy?

Could you convince someone else that they are worth pursuing?

How much do you want this dream? Enough to sustain the good times and the bad?

When would you like to achieve this first dream?

How could you modify, or change your short-term goals if there was a greater chance of achieving your long-term goal?

Who do you know who could support you?

Vision, values and beliefs

As well as encouraging learners to explore their hopes, dreams and aspirations, it is always important to help them to establish which of their overall aspirations most closely matches their personal vision, values and beliefs. Again this is an area where people will be relatively inexperienced. Encourage them to use the output from their hopes, dreams and aspirations to share their vision and again help them to make it achievable. There is no point in them setting themselves up to fail. If you encourage them to view their life as a journey, then identify their vision and short-term goals as steps along the way. Beneath the goals will be the steps that they have to take to achieve those goals and beneath the steps are the skills, knowledge and competencies required to achieve the goals.

Associated with their visions are their values and beliefs. Again this is something that is not often discussed. Goleman describes it as 'living by the inner rudder'. He describes the CEO of a utility company reserving eight hours a week for solitary reflection. In describing the 'inner rudder' further he talks about personal values being intimate credos that we may never quite articulate in words, but that we 'feel'. Self-awareness serves as an inner barometer for gauging whether what we are doing, or about to do, is indeed worthwhile.

However as Goleman points out, choices that are made in keeping with the 'inner rudder' are more energizing. People who follow their inner sense of what is worthwhile minimize emotional static for themselves. Unfortunately too many people feel that they cannot speak up for their deep values at work – that such a thing is somehow impermissible.

The rhythm and pace of modern life gives us too little time to assimilate, reflect and react. Our bodies are geared to a slower rhythm. We need time to be introspective but we don't get it, or don't take it. Self-awareness can be cultivated – by getting in touch with our deeper, quieter voice of feeling, by taking time out to 'do nothing', by not watching television but sitting quietly, meditating.

Questions

What is your short-term vision?

What is important to you?

How well do you understand your inner values? What do you believe in?

How do you make judgements?

How do you feel if your values are compromised?

Do you believe in 'putting something back' into society?

Health and personal energy, resilience, drive

Increasingly, maintaining good health is vital in people's working environment. The pace and style of work is changing; individuals need to maintain a healthy lifestyle.

Questions

What do you do to maintain good health?

What do you do to stay motivated?

How disciplined are you about taking regular exercise?

How resilient are you?

Do you view the world through a positive or a negative optic?

What are your coping strategies?

What do you do in a crisis?

Can you make things happen?

What one area would you really like to focus on improving?

Achieving life/work balance

In managing these ambitions it is important to work to achieve a balance. Many organizations are now realizing the importance of helping their employees to achieve a balance between their work and their life outside work. Encouraging your learners to take a holistic view of their lives is an important step in identifying how they can achieve this balance. This may also involve them in discussions with their partner and family about all of their long-term goals.

Too many people leave it until it is too late to start their planning for early retirement, or they discover that they have conflicting views about how and where they want to live and work. This is something that everyone should consider at an early stage in their lives, and particularly before making long-term commitments with a partner.

Managing work and life also applies to self-employed people. Individuals may have moved to pursue a more relaxed lifestyle by working for themselves and suddenly find they are working longer hours and even harder than they did when they were employed.

Questions

Which life stage have you reached? What are your future plans?

What factors may you have to consider in the future?

Can you make contingency plans to cope with these potential factors?

Have you achieved balance in your life? If yes, how will you sustain it?

If no, what could you do to make it different?

What financial implications do you have to consider? Will these change over time?

Building relationships

Organizations are beginning to recognize that managing interpersonal relationships is a core competence in their workforce. It is as relevant in the service that they provide to their customers as it is to team and line management development.

It is still one of the areas that organizations need to address because it affects everyone. The development challenge is enormous. Developing coaching skills in line managers would help the process but few organizations have really addressed the issue. Hence interpersonal relationships are often a focus of many personal coaching sessions.

Questions

How would you describe your working relationship with your line manager/team?

How do you handle difficult people/situations?

What personal impact and influence do you have, in work? Outside of work?

How well do you listen? How skilled are you at questioning?

Do you have a network of people in and out of work with whom you regularly meet?

Are your relationships healthy? How do you know?

Achieving satisfaction at work, skills, knowledge, competencies, development needs

For many people this is still an important issue. Their personal coaching focus may start in this area with their desire to improve or to develop new competencies.

Questions

How entrepreneurial are you?

Do you know your worth?

Could you convince someone else to employ you?

Do you under or over value yourself?

What are you most proud of achieving?

How relevant and up to date is your knowledge?

Who do you benchmark yourself against?

How creative do you think you are?

Do you know the role that you could play in the innovation process?

RESPONDING TO CHANGE

Opportunities to work as a personal coach with someone may be initiated as a result of an enforced change, which may be in their personal life, or at work. In their personal life this can include separation, or divorce, moving house, bereavement, health related problems, or the desire to achieve a personal ambition. At work this can mean responding to the impact of downsizing, a merger or acquisition, a new role or responsibility, a transfer to a new location, or a new boss. It may also be the desire to achieve a new qualification, or to set up on their own in business. These work-related changes can also mean that individuals think more seriously about their lifestyle options and choices; this is particularly true in the case of being made redundant, where people really reassess their options and often make major changes in the way that they live their lives. In helping individuals handle change it is important that you help them to understand the process of change and the key stages.

INITIATING CHANGE

One of the most important factors in initiating change is helping learners to explore their reasons for wanting to change. It is equally essential that the learner needs to own and want the change. As a personal coach you have to help individuals explore their options and wait while they make up their minds that they actually want that change. As discussed earlier, everyone is different and so as a coach you need to be able to help all your different learners progress at the pace and speed that suits them. As part of this process it is important that you understand the process of change.

One of the hardest parts of achieving an ambition is actually getting started. It is very easy to drift, putting off making a start. Often people use external triggers like New Year to try to start a resolution to do things differently, which is fine as long as there is a follow through strategy in place. It is not just about saying that tomorrow will be different – you need a plan to identify how you will make it different.

One of the realities in objective and goal setting is that it is all too easy to set goals and to break these goals down into SMART objectives (see Chapter 5) and yet still not to achieve anything beyond this first stage in the activity. The reason for this is that many people find it hard to kick-start themselves out of their current situation.
There are a number of reasons for this:

■ inertia;

■ fear of moving outside their own comfort zones;

■ low self-esteem;

■ workload;

■ lack of motivation, self belief;

■ lack of a real desire to do anything different.

'If you do what you always did you'll get what you always got.'

Often individuals become caught in patterns of working and behaving that are reinforced by the people and situations around them. Encouraging them to take the important first step is an essential part of the role of being a personal coach. Like any comparable form of sports or ambition coaching, it is about encouraging the individual to move forward by focusing on self-belief and taking the first tentative steps towards their goal. One other factor is to do with individual motivation. Usually what makes a significant difference in the achievement of goals is that the individual really wants to achieve them.

As they grow in confidence you can encourage them to build on SMART by setting goals which are more stretching, but in trying to help individuals to develop you need to help them achieve some success. One way of doing this is using paradigm shift.

PARADIGM SHIFT

The logic behind paradigm shift is that you are helping individuals to make a mindset change. By shifting from a negative to a positive perspective you are helping them work to achieve what they really want. This approach builds on the principles of visualization by not only helping individuals to visualize what things could be like but also moving further forward into identifying how things could feel. It can range from quite basic human activities like getting up in the morning to more personal and ambitious – for example, 'I want to be successful in achieving what I want from life.'

By shifting their personal perspectives from disbelief to belief learners can start to work to achieve what they really want. The real issue is that it is easy to say but much harder to achieve. The role of the personal coach can be to help individuals to keep reaffirming their beliefs – to help them to identify strategies for achieving the shift and to reinforce their embryonic steps towards achieving the reality. This is explored in more detail in Chapter 6. For example:

I want to get up easily in the morning = 'I enjoy getting out of bed and the beauty of mornings'

I want to be fit and healthy = 'I am a fit and healthy person'

I want to be able to network with confidence = 'People will find me interesting and stimulating'

I want to achieve my ambition = 'I have already started and am going to achieve it'

In each case the first step towards achieving a mindset change is to begin to live as if the shift had already taken place. If I want to get up easily in the morning what do I need to do to shift my perception of what enjoying getting up feels like? How could I make the mornings a more pleasant experience? If I want to be more interesting and stimulating, how would it feel to be like this and what behaviours would I need to display?

FROM DREAM TO REALITY

One of the most challenging and yet most valuable roles of a personal coach is to help learners to take control of their own destiny. One of the sad realities is that many people underachieve, often as a result of the feedback that they receive from others. Parents, teachers, friends, partners are often responsible for giving (often unsolicited) advice or feedback that so undermines a learner's confidence that they give up on a plan or course of action because of doubts fuelled by someone else. This feedback often reinforces the concerns that they may already have.

Shad Helmstetter in *What to Say When You Talk to Yourself* argues powerfully about the need to programme your brain into positive thoughts rather than the negative messages that we receive in our lives. He says that leading behavioural researchers have told us that as much as '77% of everything we think is negative and counterproductive and works against us.' He then asks

> What if each and every day, from the time you were a small child, you had been given an extra helping of self-confidence, double the amount of determination, and twice the amount of belief in the outcome? Can you imagine what tasks you might accomplish more easily, what problems you would overcome, what goals you would reach? ... Could it be that those who appear to be 'luckier' than the rest have only gotten a little better programming?... It is no longer a success theory ... The brain simply believes what you tell it most.

TEN GIFTS

As a personal coach you have a very special role. All your learners will be different and it is important to understand them fully, to identify their learning styles, to create the right learning environment for each of them and to support them in their journey towards achieving their ultimate goals. To help them there are, I believe, 10 special gifts that you might wish to share with each of them:

1. *The gift of communication*

Helping people to listen with genuine interest, to ask questions and value the responses of others.

2. *The gift of wisdom*

Encouraging learners to respect the knowledge of others, to be curious and want to share their own learning.

3. *The gift of vision*

To be able to look to the future, to chart a journey and to keep on going towards their goals.

4. *The gift of building relationships*

Being prepared to appreciate and value the contribution of others, recognizing that if we give we are more likely to receive. Develop empathy, commitment, genuine interest in others.

5. *The gift of thinking*

Help people value silence and the opportunity to reflect on their learning. Help them to understand how to think differently and to value the thought process.

6. *The gift of compassion*

Help people to want to help others help themselves, not being afraid to show they care. Being prepared to make a real contribution to their community.

7. The gift of self-belief

Help people become more self-aware and believe in themselves, to eliminate negative self-talk, to generate optimism, to take ownership of their development.

8. The gift of resilience

Help people to develop the ability to overcome setbacks and to keep going through the hard times. Learning to use failure as a stimulus to try again.

9. The gift of imagination

Help people to use their imagination to dream and see alternative ways of doing things, being innovative and creative, not being afraid to be first.

10. The gift of integrity

The ultimate gift, of connecting to their inner soul, their belief in a value system, honesty and trustworthiness.

As a personal coach the challenge is to help individual learners rise above their own negativity and to resist advice from other people until they have taken the time to really explore how they could move from dream to reality. Chapters 3 and 6 will help you identify how this can be achieved.

3

Planning the journey

One of the first stages in working with learners is to help them to identify what they really want to achieve. There can be a number of contexts for this.

It is important to help the learner work through the key stages. For some learners this may prove to be difficult if they have never had the opportunity to sit and review their hopes and dreams. Unfortunately, too often within a working environment objectives and goal setting tends to be work related – 'What are you going to do to develop competence in the areas that this organization needs?'

It will also be important to help learners to test reality. More than ever before individuals have to cope with and handle change. This was discussed in more detail in Chapter 2 but it is essential that you help your learners to really explore their options and not to make assumptions based on what has happened before. This might include helping them to make lateral moves rather than assuming that progress means promotion.

You might also work with individuals who are very happy doing what they have always done. They might not want to change. You may coach people who are suffering from a lack of confidence or self-esteem because of the feedback they have received from others in the past. Helping them to change their perspective may prove to be more of a challenge because they may see the daily actions of others reinforcing this view.

Other learners may want to develop new competencies or skills and as such you may be either directly coaching them or helping them to find the right kind of support.

If you are acting as a personal coach to an individual you can enable your learners to think about what they might want to achieve in both their work and life goals. An important first step in this is helping them to establish answers to the following:

- Where am I now?

- What would I like to do differently in the future?

- What are my work-related goals?

- What would I like to achieve outside work?

Although on the surface these are comparatively simple questions, underneath each question there is a subset of questions to enable you and the learner to identify their current situation and their future aspirations. Here are a selection of the type of questions you might ask:

- Where am I now?

- What skills and competencies have I achieved?

- What is my job role?

- What about my development on and off the job?

- Who offers me support currently?

- What would I like to do differently in the future?

- What is my style and pattern of working?

- What are my new responsibilities?

- What job change do I want?

- Do I want to transfer to another part of the business?

- What about location?

- What skills, competencies, training or new learning do I need?

- What are my work-related goals?

- In three months' time I would like to have…

- In six months' time I would like to have…

- In 12 months' time I would like to have…

- How would I break these goals down into SMART objectives?

- How could I push myself further?

- What would I like to achieve out of work?

- What are my hopes and aspirations?

- What is realistic to achieve in the short term?

- How could I break these down into bite-sized achievable goals?

- Who will offer me support?

- How will I measure my success?

One of the realities in objective and goal setting is that it is all too easy to set goals and to break these goals down into SMART objectives and yet still not to achieve anything beyond this first stage in the activity because learners may not understand their underlying motivations. This was outlined in more detail in Chapter 2.

SETTING STRETCH GOALS

Another way to help individuals to use visualization is to encourage them to set personal goals (see Chapter 5). This goal setting should be undertaken in short-, medium- and more long-term contexts. Again, help learners to succeed by encouraging them to set small targets that are achievable as well as more ambitious and long-term goals. Use techniques such as SMART and GROW (see Chapter 5) to help them identify the specifics. You might also need to have some examples to help them build their own set. By asking open questions you can help them to begin to identify the areas that they wish to work on.

As well as working through goal-setting SMART objectives and helping individual learners shift their paradigms you will also have the opportunity to work with individuals who really want to take responsibility for their own learning. They may have different motivators and drivers (see Figure 3.1).

By working through this model you can help individuals become more aware not only of their own potential but also of what they could do to accelerate their progress, or what could block their development.

One other factor is to do with individual motivation. Usually what makes a significant difference in the achievement of goals is that the individual really wants to do it. The model in Figure 3.2 illustrates one way to address this.

What is my known potential? I know I am good at this ...		What is my hidden potential? I do not know how good I could be at this, but I would like to try.	
What are my accelerators? What do I have in place to help me?	What are my blockers? What is stopping me getting what I want?	What are my accelerators? What do I have in place to help me?	What are my blockers? What is stopping me getting what I want?

Figure 3.1

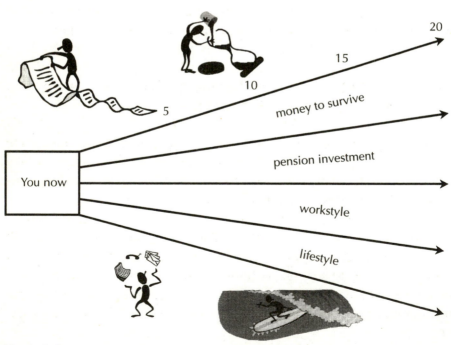

Figure 3.2

HOW MUCH MONEY DO YOU NEED TO SURVIVE?

One of the interesting points about this question is that in today's corporate society it is very easy for individuals to keep adding to their package and forget how much money they really need. It is only at times of more dramatic change, such as being made redundant or when they experience a change in their personal circumstances that they are forced to undertake a more realistic assessment of their actual financial position.

By suggesting to them that they do this analysis you help them to recognize more clearly what their options might be. You do not need to be involved but suggest that they carry it out with a financial adviser and encourage them to be realistic and to prepare for events that might happen to them later in their lives. The main reason for undertaking such an activity is that it helps them to begin to explore their options and choices. So many people make assumptions about what they can or cannot do based on inaccurate information. In this way they have a more solid foundation on which to build.

WHAT ABOUT PENSIONS, OR INVESTMENT?

The same points apply here. By highlighting them for the learner you are simply reminding them to make a provision and to start while they are young. Many people only really consider this when they are coming up to their forties or fifties and then find themselves having to work harder to make a provision. It is much better for them to consider it when they are younger because they will be building up something substantial to support them when they are older and this, in turn, could help to support them when they want to achieve a long-held hope or ambition – although, with careful planning, some ambitions can be achieved earlier and people do not need to wait until they have retired to start living the life that they really want to live.

WORKSTYLE

Your learners might never have considered their workstyle before. They might have thought about their career, they might have made choices about the type of work that they do, but actually making a choice about their workstyle might be a new step for them. The types of things to consider are based around the following.

Location of their work

Do they want to always work in the same location? Would they consider relocating? Would they ever want to work abroad? Where would they like to go? What opportunities exist within their current organization?

What restrictions could there be in their chosen country in terms of work permits and so forth? Depending on the age and experience of the individual and the country that they chose there could be a number of options open to them.

The number of hours that they are working

Some people never question the number of hours that they work. They get on a treadmill when they start work and get off at the end when they retire, unless the companies that they work for interrupt that pattern by making them redundant. Help your learners to look critically at what they do and how they do it. Ask open questions about the options that they have: their pattern of working, the time they start, the time they leave. What do they do in their lunch hour? Do they take regular breaks during the day? Do they socialize? Do they go outside and get fresh air? (Remind them about the fact that the brain uses 25 per cent of the body's oxygen, so how do they recharge their oxygen?)

Ask them to keep a journal of a typical week. What goals did they set? What did they achieve? When were they most productive? What could they have done working from home? How productive were their meetings? What could they have done differently? Helping people to challenge their assumptions about their pattern of working can be one of the most worthwhile activities you may ever undertake with them. Helping them to reassess their need to follow a set pattern can help them to free up their time so that not only can they release time for themselves but they are also more productive within their working environment.

The level of responsibility that they want

This is another area where some challenges to assumptions can be made; promotion is not necessarily the way to reward people. For many years there was a belief that career progression meant moving up an organization, taking on more and more responsibility. In recent years both individuals and organizations are beginning to realize that there are alternatives to progressing up an organization. As organizations have grown leaner, and have downsized and restructured through mergers and acquisitions, traditional career paths have changed. The development of functional specialists, the creation of new business units, the growth of internal consultants, and the impact of e-commerce have changed the face of organizational development. Helping learners to identify the level of responsibility they aspire to and looking at alternatives can be a very useful role of a personal coach. Helping them to identify how they can reduce their level of responsibility, or develop new levels of specialist skill can be part of this.

The life-stage that they have reached

As individuals move through their careers there are a number of considerations that they need to make about the life stage that they have reached and their career. The questions below illustrate some of the considerations that they need to make.

Graduate needs – first job
Have I made the right choice?
What are my options?

Can I build on them?
Do I need to change my plans?
What can this organization offer me?

Mid-twenties/thirties – second job
What new opportunities do I need?
What will I want from this job?
Am I changing direction?
Do I need retraining?
What skills am I not using?

Thirty-five/forty-five – third job
Did I get the promotion I wanted?
Is there time to change career?
What can this organization offer me?
Am I part of a succession planning process?
Do I need new skills/retraining?
Am I going anywhere?

Forty-five/fifty-five – third/fourth job
Am I gearing up or slowing down?
What do I still want to achieve?
What can I offer this organization?
What can this organization offer me?
What have I developed outside work?

Fifty-five onwards
Am I ready for retirement?
Do I want one last achievement?
Can I mentor others?
Can I construct a portfolio career?

LIFESTYLES AND WORKSTYLES

In today's working environment young people may be accelerating through a number of stages in their personal life and some of their lifestyle choices can affect this. They might also have been employed in several roles before their late twenties/thirties. Their work patterns might be quite unconventional. Obvious points around this are as follows.

At the start of their careers some people want to travel, to take time out before settling down. This sometimes occurs before they go to university, but increasingly it is an option exercised in their early twenties. Helping young learners to plan and reschedule student loans, or to identify how they will raise the finance for travelling, is an important stage for them.

As people settle and have children, the issue of mobility arises. One of the main concerns of individuals at this life stage is to help their organization recognize that if they do go through a period of limited mobility it does not necessarily mean that they never want to travel. This is often of particular concern in global organizations and leads to tensions between the organization and the individual because they are nervous of having the conversation. As people become more mature there are personal questions about what else they would like to achieve in their careers. If they take early retirement, what would that mean for them? Would they want to do something else? Work for themselves, or undertake voluntary or charity work? Fulfil a lifetime ambition?

There are an important series of questions to ask about their lifestyle. What are their hopes and aspirations? These ambitions are often linked to stages in our lives when certain things happen to us, or we reach a certain age. What is important in managing these ambitions is to work to achieve a balance. Many organizations are now realizing the importance of helping their employees to achieve a balance between their work and their life outside work. Encouraging them to take a holistic view of their lives is an important step in identifying how they can achieve this balance.

This may also involve them in discussions with their partner and family about their long-term goals. Too many people leave it until it is too late to start planning for early retirement, or they discover that they have conflicting views about how and where they want to live and work. This is something that everyone should consider at an early stage in their lives and particularly before they make long-term commitments with a partner. Managing work and life also applies to self-employed people; someone may have moved to pursue a more relaxed lifestyle by working for themselves and suddenly find that they are working longer hours and even harder than they were when they were employed.

MATCHING INDIVIDUAL AND ORGANIZATIONAL NEEDS

One of the biggest issues for individuals is time. They simply do not believe that they have the time to achieve what they want. There is also a constant juggling between what they would like to do and what they feel that they have to do, and personal development often drops down the priority order in the list. This is not just an issue for individuals: it is often reflected in the ways that organizations charge individuals with meeting business goals rather than achieving a balance between personal and organizational goals. One of the really important roles of a personal coach is to help an individual achieve a balance between their work and life goals, and to help remove the guilt that some people feel when they focus on what they might want from life. Developing a sense of their own destiny can help them to help others close to them achieve their goals too. It also has an impact on organizational development.

Many organizations still have not recognized the very real benefits of introducing coaching into the development of their managers. Developing the underpinning skills of listening, questioning, giving effective feedback, together with emotional and social competencies could have an enormous impact on business success. Some organizations appear daunted by the scale of the task of training every line manager to be a coach. However what is fundamentally important is that the development of a coaching environment has a multiplier effect. It is not just the development of a single competency. It is a real enabler, helping managers to develop their teams, not just in one skill area but many. It can also help people to be more understanding of each other, remove tensions, create a more harmonious working environment based on the development of trust and empathy and, as Ricardo Semler states in *Maverick*:

> To survive in modern times, a company must have an organisational structure that accepts change as its basic premise, lets tribal customs thrive, and fosters a power that is derived from respect, not rules. In other words, the successful companies will be the ones that put quality of life first. Do this and the rest, quality of product, productivity of workers, profits for all will follow.

4

The coaching process

This chapter is devoted to the coaching process. It is a step-by-step plan of the key stages in organizing and running a coaching meeting and, as such, underpins the rest of the chapters in this book – especially Chapter 5. It is divided into the three stages dealing with before, during and after the coaching meeting and is deliberately created as a checklist so that you can use it to ensure that you are prepared for each stage. It should be read in conjunction particularly with Chapter 5, which elaborates on the tools and techniques mentioned in this chapter. This chapter is also set into the broader context of building relationships, overcoming setbacks and focusing on the very real needs of your learner, all of which are covered in more detail in the other chapters of this book.

PRE-MEETING

Identify need for coaching:

- [ ] Agree upon the need to meet.
- [ ] Clarify the need.
- [ ] Agree date, time and place of first meeting taking account of the needs of the learner.

Prepare for coaching meeting:

- [ ] Develop a framework for the meeting – process, steps, time available and so forth.
- [ ] Prepare a list of the questions that you want to ask.
- [ ] Consider your relationship with the learner and the best way to engage them in the first meeting.
- [ ] For subsequent meetings remind yourself of what the learner was planning to achieve and their SMART objectives.

Gather background information:

☐ Copy of individual's job description (if available and appropriate – this will not be relevant in all coaching sessions; often personal coaching sits outside the normal line management, or team process).

☐ Copy of individual's latest Personal Development Review (PDR)/ action plan, again if appropriate.

☐ Any background information relating to the request for coaching.

DURING THE MEETING

Identify priorities:

☐ Having reviewed the background information, agree the specific needs for coaching with the learner.

☐ Use the models identified in Chapters 2 and 3, jointly agree priorities. Which is the most important to achieve? Where should the focus lie?

☐ Encourage the learner to make notes of their key priorities.

Use questioning and listening to explore the learner's options and choices:

☐ Use the questioning, listening and feedback techniques outlined in Chapter 5 to explore with learners what they want to achieve, or change.

☐ Each coaching session will build on the previous meeting and work through the issues and opportunities to help the learners to build their own action plans.

☐ Depending on the areas being covered progress may be made over a number of sessions and a variety of techniques may be used through the different sessions.

☐ Ideally within the first few sessions encourage the learner to set SMART objectives (see Chapter 5) that they own and that can be used as part of their action plan.

AGREE ACTION PLAN

☐ Focus on two or three key learning goals.

☐ What is the individual's preferred learning style?

☐ How will the goals be achieved – what is the learning process?

☐ What can they do for themselves? Help and support required from others?

☐ Help the individual to create a written action plan.

☐ How will progress be monitored (process, frequency and so forth)?

☐ Agree your availability for telephone/e-mail support.

☐ Agree date of next meeting.

POST-MEETING

Implement action plan:

☐ Individuals must take responsibility for implementation – it's their action plan!

☐ Encourage individuals to be realistic about what can be achieved and by when.

☐ Help them to be successful – encourage them to implement the action plan in small, manageable steps.

☐ Encourage the individual to use their network of contacts – peers, boss, subordinates and so forth for informal support/feedback.

Regularly review progress:

☐ Agree formal process dates and timings for review.

☐ Encourage learners to build progress against their objectives into their interim PDR review meetings if appropriate.

☐ Try to review once a major milestone in the action plan has been achieved and before the next one is started.

Update action plan:

☐ Help them to ensure their action plan takes account of their likely changing needs and circumstances.

☐ Always encourage learners to build an element of flexibility into their action plans.

☐ Help the learner to develop coping strategies which will enable them to overcome difficulties and setbacks (see Chapter 7).

Ongoing support:

☐ Discuss with the individual how they will continue to get help and support after the immediate coaching need has been satisfied.

Celebrate success:

☐ Help learners to review progress regularly and to recognize what they have achieved and encourage them to celebrate their real successes.

5

Personal coaching techniques

As a personal coach you will find yourself using a number of techniques, many of which are used in other applications – for example, counselling, mentoring, facilitating or managing others. What is important is the way in which you use the right techniques for the right people, and also the way in which you build the coaching relationship so that the individual is not aware that you are actually using techniques and the conversation feels natural.

A personal coach is someone with whom individual learners can develop an ongoing relationship, which enables them to explore their personal thoughts in more depth – someone who will help them to achieve insights, who will continue to be there for them over a period of time. In many ways this person is a guide, or helper, or fellow traveller. (See Figure 5.1.)

The key points about personal coaching are that when it is done well it achieves the following:

- it creates rapport;

- it creates the right environment;

- it is part of an ongoing relationship;

- it focuses on the individual;

- it enables both participants to share mutual respect and gives them an opportunity to learn from each other;

- it enables them to apply higher level skills/competencies;

- actions are agreed upon and followed through.

CREATING RAPPORT

Being natural is an essential part of building relationships with others and where there is understanding and mutual respect even minimal communication will be effective. A glance across a crowded room can convey a clear message between two people where there is already rapport. Tuning into someone else's moods, interest level and underlying

They normally want to do something different in their lives, in work, or outside.
They usually either want a new skill, knowledge, or to fulfil an ambition. Sometimes they also want to support ,or do something for someone else.
With the overall outcome of personal satisfaction, sense of achievement, happiness for themselves, or others.
How will they achieve it? Application of the personal coaching process: 'what?' 'why?' 'when?' 'where?' 'how?'
Followed by identification of how they will meet their goals and objectives and achieve their action and development plan.
Stimulated by a generous application of personal motivation, drive and desire to really want to make it happen and to overcome setbacks.
Supported with a careful process of support and challenge from their personal coach and their network of friends, family and colleagues.
Followed by regular ongoing review of progress together with celebration of success.

Figure 5.1 Why would a learner want to use a personal coach?

needs is an important part of creating rapport. Even if someone does not naturally relate to others, the skilled communicators can find meeting points where they can engage the interest of others.

THE RIGHT ENVIRONMENT

One of the potential disadvantages with the growth of more technology-based learning is the lack of human contact. Individual learners can lose the opportunity to talk through their embryonic ideas with other people. The whole philosophy of self-managed learning provides individuals with choices about how and where they learn, which has distinct advantages for both the individual and the organization. However one of the potential losses from the reduction in training programmes is not so much what happens in the classroom, or lecture theatre but the reduction in the learning that takes place on training events in those quieter, more intimate moments when two people start talking to each other at the end of a day, or in seminar groups before someone interrupts and tells them to get on with the task.

If you have ever been trained to coach you will know the importance of creating the right environment. However what this normally means is making sure that there are not desks, tables or other barriers between you and the person you are coaching. Environment can also mean thinking outside the normal educational or corporate confines of training and development.

> Picture the scene, two people sitting outside deep in conversation, relaxing with refreshments readily available. In front of them the countryside rolls away bathed in the afternoon sunshine. Across in the main building two people stretch out in the sauna, while yet another is swimming, to the unfocused eye this could be seen purely as a leisure-time activity. To the experienced personal coach this will be recognised as an opportunity for some of the most powerful learning to take place.

This extract taken from Thorne and Machray (2000) highlights the importance of creating environments where people can relate to each other in an unhurried relaxed way. Create the right environment and the learning really becomes much more profound.

AN ONGOING RELATIONSHIP

One of the values of this approach is that this relationship can endure over time. Part of the initial conversation is about sharing background information about each other, and this information is built on each time that the pair meet. In this way the conversation can be picked up and put down over a period of time but the richness of knowledge grows deeper through the ongoing nature of the relationship. What characterizes the nature of this relationship are the following:

- responsiveness;

- trust;

- confidentiality;

- shared responsibility;

- honesty;

- open responses;

- commitment to make it work.

These are the very things that are essential in all good relationships.

FOCUS ON THE INDIVIDUAL

Many people do not respond naturally in groups. Peer influence and fixed ideas about how they should behave, all serve to reduce the effectiveness of individuals within group work activities and discussions. It is very important to allow people the opportunity to be themselves and to experience personal growth. Having achieved the position of being comfortable with themselves and confident in the way that they articulate their hopes, dreams and aspirations they are much better able to communicate this to others.

SHARING MUTUAL RESPECT AND THE OPPORTUNITY TO LEARN FROM EACH OTHER

One of the most significant factors in the history of recent times is the introduction of new technology. The speed of this development has meant dramatic changes in global markets and in what is perceived as valuable knowledge acquisition. Maturity and length of time served no longer mean automatic status in an organization.

Respect has to be earned and the sharing of expertise can move across generations. The elderly can learn from the young and vice-versa. Everyone has the opportunity to develop conversations with a number of people. These are selected based on the desire to learn from each other and shared interest, and increasingly a desire to spend time with each other. Time for conversations initially may be at a premium and so the very nature of choosing who you want to spend time with becomes increasingly important. Equally, because there is freedom of choice, meetings are set up by mutual agreement. In some cases this may happen outside the working environment. If people perceive it to be of value, then they will make time for it. What can also happen is that people can have a number of people with whom they meet, sharing different conversations and so widening and enriching the experience.

A skilled personal coach will help individuals develop their networks so that they can have a richness of communication with a number of people.

APPLICATION OF HIGHER SKILLS/COMPETENCIES

As highlighted a number of times in this book, it is the naturalness of the conversation and the relationship that can often be most powerful and although, on the surface, this approach could be viewed as being too casual or informal, in fact the underpinning application involves high levels of listening, questioning and giving feedback. The difference is that the more natural the environment, the longer the relationship, the deeper the understanding.

At first the meetings may seem to be unstructured. However, over a period of time it is likely that a pattern will evolve and a framework will be agreed.

ACTIONS ARE AGREED UPON AND FOLLOWED UP

As mentioned above it is very easy to meet, to have a great conversation, full of richness, to both agree to do things and then to meet again, possibly several weeks later, and find that nothing has happened. In some circumstances that may be the right outcome because the individual learner needs reflection time. However, agreeing ground rules about follow up, or committing to find out further information before the next meeting, or sending information to each other, can enrich the overall experience.

RIGHT TIME, RIGHT PLACE, RIGHT PERSON

The hidden message from my school, I eventually realized, was not only crippling it was wrong. The world is not an unsolved puzzle, waiting for the occasional genius to unlock its secrets. The world, or most of it, is an empty space waiting to be filled. That realization changed my life. I did not have to wait and watch for the puzzles to be solved, I could jump into the space myself. I was free to try out my ideas, invent my own scenarios, create my own futures.

(Handy, 1995)

This does not just apply to the development of your skills as a personal coach it is also relevant to your own learning. Skilled partners will delight in your learning; they will help you to move forward with encouragement, giving you positive feedback .What distinguishes the experience is that it is different, it is memorable and it forms an important part of your development. Find the right time, the right place and the right person to guide your personal understanding and it will enable you to experience learning which is so profound that the memory will stay with you forever.

WHAT IS DIFFERENT ABOUT PERSONAL COACHING?

The difference about personal coaching is exactly that it is personal and as such it should focus completely on the individual learner. You can also help learners to understand how they relate to others and, importantly, why that interconnectivity works better with some people rather than others. As well as enabling the learner to discover their uniqueness you can also help them on their journey to discover the uniqueness of others and how to both enjoy and reflect on the synergy of their relationships with others with whom they can develop trust. It has been mentioned several times in this book that the better you know yourself, the better able you are to develop healthy relationships with others.

ATTRIBUTES OF GOOD COACHES

- They are trusted and respected.

- They role model behaviour and live the values.

- They have relevant experience, which adds value.

- They have good communication skills – they question, build, clarify, summarize.

- They offer encouragement and support.

- They take time to listen.

- They let people figure things out for themselves.

- They work in partnership.

- They have a strong belief that improvement is always possible.

- They focus on an end goal.

- They take joint responsibility for the outcome.

THE ROLE OF COACHES

- They build a positive environment.
- They ask questions to analyse needs.
- They use open questions to probe.
- They focus on the needs of the individual.
- They offer suggestions to build on views expressed by learners.
- They listen actively.
- They seek ideas and build on them.
- They give feedback.
- They agree action plans for development.
- They monitor performance.
- They give ongoing support.
- They focus on improving performance in the current job.
- They assist in raising performance to required standards.
- They emphasize the present.

The importance of client confidentiality, not mistaking coaching for counselling and only undertaking coaching if you are competent to do so cannot be stressed enough. The techniques highlighted in this chapter are only the first step to you taking your own development much further through learning and coaching until you develop your own competence.

CODE OF PRACTICE

It is important that you should also establish your own personal code of practice. For example:

- Respect confidentiality at all times.

- Respond by coaching, not counselling.

- Work to create a supportive and appropriately challenging environment.

- Be prepared to build an enduring relationship with the learner.

- Equally be prepared to end the relationship and/or refer on to someone else if you and the learner feel it is appropriate.

- Focus on a holistic view.

- Have the desire to want to model and challenge your own development.

- Be curious – stimulate curiosity in your learner.

- Recognize that the individual is in charge of their own destiny.

This is only a starting point. Think very carefully about what you would like to have in your own code of practice. Personal coaching is also set within the broader context of other types of coaching:

- Coaching for development:
  - focusing on growth for additional challenge/responsibility;
  - starting from a baseline of acceptable performance;
  - emphasis on future career;
  - developing individuals beyond the required standard or for broader career development.
- Coaching for performance:
  - helping individuals to reach the required standard;

– acknowledging and agreeing aspects of performance to work on;

– discussing work on performance;

– reviewing job elements and deliverables.

BUILDING A COACHING RELATIONSHIP

The first step

To enable yourself to create a memorable learning experience you need to identify your own skill set and levels of competence. At the end of this chapter is a self-assessment pro-forma to help you identify areas that you may wish to focus on in your own development plan. Below is an examination of some of the activities that you may wish to consider based on the steps as identified at the start of this chapter.

Creating rapport

Being natural was highlighted as one of the essential parts of building a relationship. Think about your own style and the way that you build relationships. Ask yourself how comfortable you are when you are building relationships with others. Are you aware of your personal impact?

Creating the right environment

Thinking about creating the right environment for the learner is an important part of the role of a personal coach. Take every opportunity to create environments that are outside the confines of work. Try to think creatively.

Personal coaching does not always have to take place inside: you can walk and talk! Think about places that provide inspiration. Combine visiting somewhere followed by a quiet time sitting and talking over a meal, or coffee.

The ownership of action will lie with the individual. Having a small pad for jotting notes, or a hand-held electronic notebook, means that you have immense freedom not to be stuck in a corporate office. Spend time at the start of the relationship exploring different options; seek to understand where the learner may feel more comfortable. Initially it may take time before the learner feels comfortable in a different environment. Always have a settling-in period. The more natural you are, the more attuned they become towards their surroundings and the better the foundation on which to build the relationship. Remember the information in Chapter 2 about recognizing the needs of the individual. Individual learners will respond differently to different environments.

Always be sensitive to their needs and, although the environment may be more informal, never compromise on your professionalism or integrity.

Building an ongoing relationship

All the best learning takes place when a climate of trust between the learner and the developer is created; but personal coaching, unlike some other forms of training or learning, endures over time. As a result there needs to be an even greater focus on building a trusting and honest environment. As the personal coach you need to be reassuring about confidentiality, highly responsive and seek to encourage learners to take personal ownership, to be open in their responses and to have a commitment to make it work.

Ask yourself the following questions:

- Do we value each other?

- Have we created an environment of trust?

- Is there a commitment to make it work?

Being focused on the individual

This builds on the section above, but one of the major advantages of personal coaching is that it is about developing a one-to-one relationship where the individual feels able to articulate and explore their hopes, fears and aspirations. When you are exploring their needs remember the importance of the inner and outer ring in Figure 2.1. As well as an assessment of the skills, knowledge and competencies that they may wish to develop, encourage them to consider their emotional and social competencies as defined by Goleman:

■ self-awareness;

■ self-regulation;

■ motivation;

■ empathy;

■ social skills.

For full details of the competencies see Goleman (1999).

You and your learners will find it invaluable if you encourage them to use some kind of preference or profiling tools. Gaining personal insight is a crucial part of focusing on the individual. Encourage them to recognize how the different components of their own personal jigsaws fit together. Encourage them to be curious and intrigued about how they impact on others. Hold up the mirror and allow them to reflect on who they are, remember the 'inner rudder' as discussed in Chapter 2. Help them to articulate their beliefs and values. Help them to understand how they can create their own value system and apply it to their life in and out of work. Help them to recognize the importance of emotional and social competencies.

Share mutual respect and learn from each other

One of the significant parts of a personal coaching relationship is helping individuals value their own experience, skills and personal attributes. Encouraging them to share this knowledge and feel valued for what they know is an important part of the relationship. This has particular relevance when you are coaching more experienced individuals. Show genuine interest, encourage them to be proud of their knowledge and expertise. So many individuals have received more negative than positive feedback in their careers. Encourage them to build their self-esteem and acceptance of praise for achievements through setting SMART goals and then celebrating success. One important part of this is the development of a network, encouraging them to take the opportunities of meeting with a wide circle of people. It may also be about encouraging them to share their expertise more formally, possibly through making presentations, talking to interested groups, and sharing their knowledge and experiences both in and out of work.

Application of higher skills/competencies

When was the last time you really listened to someone properly? How well do you listen? Do you really suspend your prejudices and listen to others with your whole mind? Often people are thinking about what they are going to say next, or making assumptions about the individual, or worse still thinking about something completely different. Have you developed the skill of effective questioning? Have you developed the ability to ask open questions, to create a natural conversational style, when you are able to ask significant questions by following a process of careful probing? The most skilled interviewers, coaches and conversationalists have incredibly enhanced skills of questioning, listening and observing and consequently people relax and are willing to talk to them. The opposite of this is when people unskilled in questioning and listening clumsily work their way through a process, trying to remember what is an open question and in their concern to get it right make the conversations stilted and unnatural.

One way of developing the skills of both questioning and listening is to practise it as often as possible. All the skills involved in personal coaching are based on natural behaviours: showing genuine interest, having normal conversations with people. One of the critical actions is to ask a question and then wait for a response. So often people ask a question and then either think about the next question or allow their minds to wander rather than really listening to the answer and then formulating their response to the next question.

Doing it properly takes time, but the value to your learner is almost beyond measure. Another useful activity is to watch other people, colleagues, people you meet socially, at events, on television. Spend a few moments thinking about the people who you enjoy talking to, analyse exactly what they do that you like. Think about your own style: what do you need to focus on? The self-assessment at the end of this chapter can help you to review the way you question and listen to others.

Actions agreed and followed up

As a personal coach the action planning part of the relationship is a very important stage. You may have worked really well with your learner, there may have been a rich and deep conversation and you may have used a high level skill-set of questioning and listening, but what happens next is equally important.

It is important that the individual learner takes ownership, but also that you support the process. When you are working closely with someone there is a different level of responsibility related to a duty of care to help learners think really carefully through their next steps.

It is all too easy for a learner unused to decision making to set out on a journey that they are unprepared for simply as a result of a conversation. Informally and socially this can happen all too frequently when an individual talks through an issue with some of their friends or colleagues and based on the consensus viewpoint makes important decisions which they may later come to regret.

As a personal coach one of your roles is to help individual learners really think through the consequences of their actions and also to help them set up a clear process for identifying and achieving their objectives. There is also a useful question to ask when all the analysis has taken place and a decision has been made, which is 'Do you still really want to do this?' Whatever action is required, people do sometimes change their minds but may find it difficult to get off a train of activity that is gathering momentum. Encouraging them to review carefully at each stage of their progress against their original objectives, and helping them to refine them if necessary, is one way to ensure that, when they achieve their goals, they still want them.

Staying in touch through phone calls and/or e-mails is another way to provide ongoing support and is an important part of being a personal coach.

Right time, right place and right person

This is the personification of the ideal coaching relationship for both the coach and the learner. If you want to create memorable learning experiences you need to give them your full attention. You cannot coach half-heartedly and expect to create a memorable learning experience. It does take the application of higher skills – it does mean thinking carefully about how you structure the learning sessions and it does mean devoting real time and attention to the learner, but when you achieve all this the learning will be very special.

SPECIFIC TOOLS AND TECHNIQUES

In Chapter 4 the coaching process was outlined, the following sections refer to some of the techniques that will help you and your learner gain the most from the coaching experience.

QUESTIONING

As stated frequently throughout this book, the ability to ask the right question at the right time is a fundamental part of effective coaching. Normally there should be an overall pattern to the questioning process but, as well as acknowledging this pattern, it is also important that the conversation is as natural as possible, so recognize the process, understand it, absorb it and then use it naturally.

Types of questions

Closed questions ask for precise, normally short answers – often 'yes' or 'no'. They are used to agree the rules at the start of a conversation, to search for agreement during a conversation and to confirm agreement at the end of a conversation. Open questions begin with: 'how', 'why', 'when', 'who', 'where'… Most of a conversation is built around open questions.

Pattern of questioning through a coaching meeting

The coaching meeting will be structured around a pattern of questioning that is designed to help you and the learner to manage the time available in a way that helps the learner to settle into the meeting, explore options and choices and leave feeling that there is a sense of completeness about the meeting. Being aware of the time available and fitting the questioning process into the time available are equally important.

To settle the learner ask questions based on factual information which they can easily respond to. These may be closed, 'yes/no' responses or simple open questions such as:

- Did you drive here?

- We have a three-hour session?

- Would you like a coffee before we start?

Once they have settled, start to review the last session or, if this is the first meeting, explore their reasons for wanting personal coaching asking broad, open-ended general questions such as:

■ You were going to contact that agency; how did you get on?

■ What was the outcome of the meeting with John?

■ Did you address the issues that you wanted to raise?

As the meeting develops you should find yourself asking more open and deeper probing questions such as:

■ What are your options?

■ How would you like it to be different?

■ Why do you feel like that?

You will find times when you may need to ask clarifying questions by asking questions to check your understanding, or to gain more information such as 'Tell me more about the situation' and 'What exactly do you mean by that?'

It is important to ask questions carefully, recognizing that as you probe you may touch on very sensitive areas for an individual, which may relate to incidents in their past that may trigger their emotions. Again recognize the importance of the difference between coaching and counselling. If you do trigger an emotion, allow the learner time to recover, suggest a coffee, or a short break and when you resume be very careful how you proceed. You may also choose to suggest that they may want to talk the issue through with someone who is a trained counsellor.

Towards the end of the meeting, or at stages during the meeting, it will be helpful to your learners to assist them to summarize the stage reached with either statements or questions:

- So what are the decisions you have made?

- What are you going to do before our next meeting?

- How will you know you've been successful?

Whenever you ask questions always wait for their response, do not confuse them by asking multiple questions. Do not be afraid of silence. The nature of personal coaching is that learners will sometimes need time to reflect, or they may hesitate before replying. If you jump in and fill the space you may never get their true and most honest responses. Silence might encourage a further, deeper response. You should also take time to analyse the response and to frame your next question.

At the end of the session allow time for the learner to 'cool down' in the same way as in a fitness session. Recognize that the meeting is coming to a close and revert to the same style of questions that you used at the start of the meeting. Be more conversational, ask about where the learner may be going next, make sure that you agree the next stage – actions, or the time of the next meeting if appropriate. Do not attempt to ask deep and probing questions at this stage as it is unlikely that there will be enough time to address the issues that they might wish to raise. Make sure that they are fully relaxed and ready to leave. If it has been a particularly thought-provoking session you may want to reinforce the fact that they can contact you in between sessions if they want to discuss a key point.

As well as asking effective questions it is equally important to be able to listen properly. Very few people are really good listeners, it is so easy to find yourself thinking your own thoughts, preparing for the next question. There are a number of things that you can do to help yourself to listen.

There are some physical and mental actions that you can use to demonstrate attentiveness:

Physically:

- face the speaker;
- maintain eye contact;
- keep an open posture;
- lean towards the speaker;
- stay relaxed;
- don't interrupt;
- watch the non-verbal signs.

Mentally:

- listen for the central theme;
- keep an open mind;
- think ahead;
- analyse what is being said;
- listen to words and feelings;
- listen to what is not being said.

GIVING FEEDBACK

As well as questioning and listening there will be occasions when you will need to give feedback and for the learner it will be absolutely critical to get it right. So often the feedback that individuals may have received in their lives may not have been given in a sensitive and skilled manner. The nature of your relationship is such that you need to think very carefully about how you can help your learner not just to receive but also to give feedback.

- Prepare carefully, think around the situation, think about how learners might respond.

- Always ask for their view first – it will give you a starting point.

- Always start with the positive.

- Ask questions; listen to the responses.

- Give specific examples as part of the feedback.

- Make helpful suggestions for improvement.

- Check the learners' understanding and agreement.

- Offer help and support.

- Always end on a positive and upbeat note.

Summarize the feedback and agree the next steps. If there is something that they want to work on agree a timetable for review.

SMART

The acronym SMART usually stands for: 'Specific, Measurable, Achievable, Realistic, Timed'. It is a technique used in both training and coaching to help a learner set very specific objectives.

Specific

What is it exactly that your learner wants to achieve? Can they write it in one sentence? If they can't, can they summarize the broad parameters? If they have several goals, can they prioritize in order of either time or importance?

Measurable

How will they know that they have achieved it? Can they write some measures of success?

Achievable

This is one of the most important tests of an objective. If it is not achievable then the learner is likely to become really demotivated and if it is not achievable why are they setting themselves up for failure? In this section it is also important to recognize that the objective may need to be achievable over a period of time, or through a number of steps. Sometimes learners may have to set themselves short-term goals to help them achieve the bigger goal.

Realistic

This is perhaps one of the most important steps. This moves a goal from fantasy to reality. It is no good the learner setting themselves goals that are totally unrealistic. This isn't about not setting over challenging goals, but more about adopting a common sense approach.

One of the failings of some motivational texts is that they encourage people to try to achieve the impossible. While for some this may prove to be the very trigger that sets them on their way, for many their hopes and dreams need a surer foundation. By setting realistic objectives the learner minimizes the risk of backing out.

Timed

The learner can help the achievement of their objectives by setting a timeline over which they hope to achieve their goals.

GROW

Another technique is GROW which stands for:

Goals:

- What are the SMART (Specific, Measurable, Achievable, Realistic, Timed) goals? What exactly do you want to achieve?
- Why are you hoping to achieve this goal?
- What are the expectations of others?
- Who else needs to know about your plan? How will you inform them?

Reality:

- What is the reality of the current situation?
- Why haven't you reached this goal already?
- What is really stopping you?
- Do you know anyone who has achieved this goal?
- What can you learn from them?

Options:

- What could you do as a first step?
- What else could you do?
- Who do you know who has done it differently?
- What could you learn from them?
- What would happen if you did nothing?

Will:

- Where does this goal fit in with your personal priorities at present?

- Do you have other priorities which are taking your energy and motivation?

- What obstacles do you expect to meet? How will you overcome them?

- How would you score your level of commitment on a scale of 0–10?

- If your commitment score is less than 8 will you actually get started?

- Do you really want to do it?

- If yes, when are you going to start?

(Adapted from Whitmore, 1996.)

SWOT

Strengths, Weaknesses, Opportunities, Threats.

This is a way to add structure to a brainstorm, and like some of the techniques identified earlier in this book can be used to help the learner explore their options. Strengths and weaknesses are often perceived as current and internal issues and opportunities and threats as future and external issues.

SWOT can be applied to any number of situations in the learner's working or non-working life. It can be something that they may start on their own and then share with their partner, manager, team or colleagues. A personal coach can help probe some of their assumptions.

MIND MAPPING

One of the most creative and enjoyable ways of generating ideas is Mind Maps®, invented by Tony Buzan. His work is related to the development of whole-brain thinking and encourages learners, through the use of words and images, to create a map of what they want to focus on. The advantage of both SWOT and mind mapping is that large amounts of information can be summarized on one page. These techniques, together with SMART and GROW, provide a structure to help you work with the learner to achieve their goals and objectives. Again, they should be incorporated into the overall coaching process.

As well as the techniques described above there are a number of other techniques that you may wish to find out more about and identify if they are useful to you in your role as a personal coach. In each case there is not enough space in this book to do full justice to the depth and application of the learning, so they are merely summarized. If you want to use any of them with a learner it is important that you first learn and develop your own skill set. As mentioned previously, your learner should not become the focus of your experiments. You first need to develop your own full understanding and in some cases become a registered practitioner before using the techniques with others.

STORYTELLING

One of the most valuable thoughts behind this approach is its enduring nature; if we look back through history, much learning took place at the feet of 'elders' – wise people who shared their wisdom with young scholars through talking to them. All the great cultures have used storytellers to communicate messages of bravery and to unify and stabilize communities.

> From time to time [the] tribe [gathered in a circle]. They just talked and talked and talked, apparently to no purpose. They made no decisions. There was no leader. And everybody could participate. They may have been wise men, or wise women who were listened to a bit more – the older ones, but everybody could talk. The meeting went on, until it finally seemed to stop for no reason at all and the group dispersed. Yet after that everybody seemed to know what to do, because they understood each other so well. Then they could get together in smaller groups and do something, or decide things.
>
> (David Bohm, quoted in Jaworski, 1998)

Storytelling is a way of passing on history, but is also has modern-day applications. We are all storytellers. It can be a powerful tool. You can attend courses, which are dedicated to the art of storytelling. Storytelling is normally a 'live' experience, either in front of a real audience on a stage, or as part of a small group. The story is also normally told rather than read, using the magical capacity of a story told around a fire when the storyteller is skilled in the ability of good storytelling.

VISUALIZATION

Visualization is another technique that has been around for centuries. It is about the ability to visualize an image and believe that you can achieve it. It is about helping the learner believe that it is possible to change and break old habits. It is about focusing on what learners really want to achieve and helping them not just to see the picture but to really believe that they can achieve it.

Whatever your learners want to achieve it is important that they can clearly visualize it. Some people write it down and keep the piece of paper with them; some display their goals by having visual images that illustrate what they are trying to achieve. It is important to keep visualizing their goals and to think about them in a positive way. Equally, others create their own special tapes of inspirational music to help them maintain their momentum. They need to keep revisiting it and nurturing it. The more they reinforce it the closer it will become. In this way it is similar to the paradigm shift mentioned earlier in this book. By visualizing what you want to achieve you can develop a series of positive affirmations that this is what you really want. This process is often used in sports coaching: individuals or teams are encouraged to visualize their success. They are encouraged to imagine the emotion, the sense of success, the sounds and the inner passion and drive to achieve them.

NEURO-LINGUISTIC PROGRAMMING (NLP)

Neuro-linguistic programming is similar to visualization. It was started in the 1970s by John Grinder and Richard Bandler. The 'neuro' part of NLP refers to the neurological processes of seeing, hearing, feeling, tasting and smelling – our senses. The 'linguistic' part refers to the importance of language in our thought processes and our communication, for example:

- Visual: we think in pictures – ideas, memory and imagination are mental images.

- Auditory: we think in sounds. These sounds could be voices, or noises of everyday sounds.

- Feelings: we represent sounds as feelings that might be internal emotion or the thought of physical touch. Taste and smell are often in this category.

'Programming' refers to the way that we can programme our own thoughts and behaviour like the way a computer is programmed to do specific tasks.

Neuro-linguistic programming is a practical technique concerned with outcomes and has developed the concept of modelling excellent performance. As well as helping you to build your own skill set, NLP has a number of applications within organizations – for example in customer services and in helping people to communicate more effectively. It can underpin visualization by helping a learner to reprogramme from acceptance of failure to belief in success (see Chapter 9).

Further details of these techniques can be found in the books listed in the Bibliography (for example O'Connor and Seymour, 1990, 1994).

6

Doing it differently

EXPLORING OTHER WAYS OF WORKING

This chapter is about helping you to work with people who will respond to different approaches. As discussed in earlier chapters everyone is different and those who are particularly imaginative and creative may need additional support in helping them to achieve their full potential.

As a personal coach you will work with people with a wide range of profiles and work preferences. Some people may think more laterally than others and as such may need support to help them think through their ideas. They may also need coaching to help them position their ideas and influence others.

The spectrum of creativity spans from idea generation through to implementation and individuals will have different preferences. For example, people who are idea generators will tend to need support in positioning their ideas within the organization and also how to find people who can support them in the implementation. Those who are explorers of concepts may need encouragement to help them to move forward and not to confuse others by adding yet another spin to an idea.

Someone who responds better to generating ideas with others needs to recognize how to identify people whom they can discuss ideas with. People who are natural implementers will need support to prevent them simply 'thinking and doing' without qualifying or evaluating their ideas.

Others may describe themselves as not being creative and as a result will need support to help them to recognize that they do have a role to play in the creative process.

By working with each individual you can help people to think differently about the opportunities that are presented to them and about how to build on their natural preferences. It is important to help people who are naturally creative to handle their creativity because these people may find it a challenge fitting into traditional organizational structures and as a result may be perceived as being 'difficult'.

IDENTIFYING SOURCES OF INSPIRATION

If you are a trainer, teacher or coach you may spend almost all of your working life helping others to soar, but what about you? When was the last time that you thought about your own hopes, dreams and ambitions?

If you want to learn how to soar, before you take off you need to draw on your innate wisdom about yourself and to really explore your potential to help you reach your greatest heights.

How well do you know yourself? How far do you push the boundaries of discovery? What do you do to inspire yourself?

Inspiration is sometimes hard to define. You cannot easily anchor it down and look at it. It is a sense, a feeling, a mood, something that lifts you above the ordinary and enables you to achieve something special. To be inspired transcends the normal day-to-day activities. People who are inspired have a special ability. However well motivated you are there may be times when you need to recharge, or to be inspired to enable you to work more effectively with others.

Mihaly Csikszentmihalyi, a University of Chicago psychologist, has undertaken a number of studies into the process called 'flow'. He says that we experience 'flow' when we feel in control of our actions and are masters of our own fate. What he discovered was that when people were experiencing 'flow' their state was very similar – there was a sensation of pleasure, they felt as if they were floating, they were totally immersed in what they were doing, they forgot their worries and lost sense of time.

One of the challenges is to focus because so many thoughts come floating into your mind that it can be difficult to capture them all. Many people feel that their best ideas occur when they are least expecting it, or doing something else. However once the ideas start to flow you want to try to capture them. It is also important to record everything, as even the most insignificant points may ultimately become important features of the end result.

Equally, if you find that the ideas are not flowing it is important not to force the process. It is better to leave it and do something else. Often people find that by doing something completely different their mind will suddenly start generating ideas. Creative thinking also takes place at night through something called the theta process, which is when the mind produces its own solutions that are there when you awake. If you expose yourself to richness of experience you can stimulate your creativity by drawing down from external stimuli and other pleasurable experiences.

When you are coaching others take time to help them explore their own creativity, use a variety of sources to help them recognize the rich variety of ways of doing things differently.

SYNCHRONICITY

Synchronicity: The inner path of leadership, by Joseph Jaworski (1998), is a very thoughtful book written about the release of human potential. Jaworski talks about 'a fundamental shift of mind' and:

> operating in this different state of mind and being, we come to a very different sense of what it means to be committed...When this new type of commitment starts to operate, there is a flow around us. Things just seem to happen...When we are in a state of commitment and surrender, we begin to experience what is sometimes called 'synchronicity'.

Trying to define synchronicity can be very complex or very simple, Jung defined it as 'a meaningful coincidence of two or more events, where something other than the probability of chance is involved.' Peter Senge, writing in the introduction to Jaworski's book, warns of the dangers of trying to control synchronicity in the same way that we might try to control the rest of our lives. He says that:

> people tend to elevate synchronicity into a sort of magical mystical experience. In fact it is very down to earth. Water flows downhill because of gravity...we don't argue about the result because it's observable. That's much the same way that synchronicity seems to operate in this field of deep commitment.

James Redfield (1998) in *The Celestine Vision* states:

> The most important key in learning to take advantage of the various synchronicities in our lives is to stay alert, and make the time necessary to explore what is occurring. In order to do this, each of us needs to create in our life a sufficient amount of what I call drift time – time when we are doing nothing but hanging out, flipping through the newspaper, or walking down the street alert to what is around us. If you think of a friend drop by, see what happens.

You may have already experienced one of those moments when you are searching for something and suddenly you meet someone, or read something and it takes your breath away, because it is an expression of your innermost thoughts, or it is a solution presented at the very moment you needed it.

If you are acting as a personal coach for learners it is important that you help them explore all the options open to them, but also help them to open their eyes so that they see things that they might normally ignore. Encourage them to be curious, to have an openness and desire to find out more. In today's society, more than ever before, there is a critical need for knowledge management. With the advent of the Internet and the speed of technological development it is even more essential to have some kind of mechanism to help you sift and identify what is important and relevant and what to ignore. Just like the saying 'you don't know what you don't know' you can waste vast amounts of time searching for what you think you might find. Life is a bit like that; without an overall vision it is so easy to be overwhelmed by other people, situations, or too much information.

Having a personal vision enables you to edit out what is irrelevant. It makes sense of 'working smarter not harder'. It also means that you have time to explore what is really important for you, your partner, your family and those you want to work or live with in your local community. This equally applies to your learners – help them to develop the attributes in Figure 6.1.

Be there for them – help them to work through the stages and help them to develop the underpinning skill set.

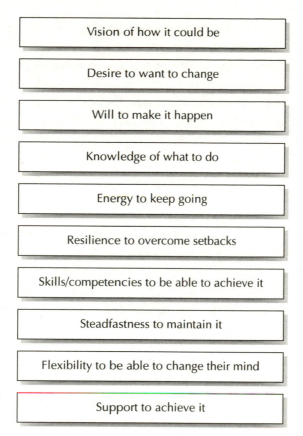

Figure 6.1 Initiating change

Equally help them to recognize the following. From time to time we will experience situations, meetings, things we read that have a fundamental, or profound effect on us. This is often described as 'right place, right time, with the right people'. Equally we might experience periods of time when we feel unable to move forward because, as we describe it, 'the timing is not right'.

As individual learners help them to gain the courage to go with the opportunities that are presented to them, do not encourage them to take foolish risks, but help them to manage risk, and use it to their advantage.

You are never too old or too young to recognize what potential you may have. It is, however, very easy to ignore your talents, or to be put off from doing something today and to carry on doing what you have always done.

There are enough distractions, enough good reasons for individuals never to realize their ambitions. The world is full of people who will discourage them, fill them with self-doubt, or simply make too many demands on their time.

If you expose yourself to richness of experience you can stimulate your creativity by drawing down from external stimuli and other pleasurable experiences. When you find that your creativity is being stifled take a break, and do something completely different. Take regular time out to indulge yourself. Use others for support. Bounce ideas, however crazy; build on initial fleeting thoughts to anchor more tangible concepts. You need to keep inspired so that you can inspire others. Help your learner to unlearn lessons from childhood, to say 'I can' instead of 'I can't'.

POSITIVE THINKING

Most people are aware of the phrase 'half full, or half empty' referring to the way that people perceive a glass filled half way. The optimists traditionally will perceive the glass as half-full. The pessimists will view it as being half empty. An individual's approach to life may be very much built on the same premise. If people view life from a negative perspective the personal coach can help them to construct the steps towards a more positive perspective. This is not necessarily an easy task because you may well be working against a background of long-standing views. In this context the coach can work with individuals to help them take small steps towards a different view. For example, see the manager-and-his-team scenario below.

Some possible questions could be:

- 'What don't you like about the current meetings?'
- 'What would you like to be different in the meetings?'

- 'If you could change one thing about the way you interact with the group what would it be?'

Start by identifying a particular situation and ask them to describe their view of what happened. Listen carefully to the language that they use; identify the words, categorize them under + and – headings. For example, an individual might say 'Today I had a meeting with my team and I got really fed up because they wouldn't take responsibility for anything':

+	–
	fed up
	they wouldn't take responsibility

The coach asks further probing questions such as 'What were the positive actions that were agreed?' The individual responds 'Well there weren't any – they just kept avoiding the issues and made me so angry that I ended up saying that I would follow up on the actions.'

+	–
	they kept avoiding the issues
	they made me so angry that I ended up
	agreeing to do it instead.

The coach asks 'What could you do differently next time?' The individual responds 'I don't know. It happens every time, they are incapable of doing things on time, so I end up taking the tasks back again.'

+	–
	it happens every time
	they are incapable
	I end up taking the tasks back again.

This dialogue could continue but the pattern is established, if you review the above sentences you will see the argument becomes a circular one: *'They* won't, so *I must.'* Although this example may be extreme it illustrates a number of important points:

■ there are many references to *they;*

■ there is an emphasis on powerlessness – *they make me;*

■ there is equally an assumption of responsibility *they won't so I must.*

The perspective is one of anger, frustration and blame. This situation is damaging for everyone.

Helping this particular manager to shift perspective will take time and careful support and there is no guarantee of success. As a personal coach working with a manager in this situation it is essential to help him recognize his starting point. Gently helping him to review a scenario like the one above will involve enabling him to analyse what happened and to explore some 'what if' alternatives. For example one could ask the following questions:

■ How well do you know your team?

■ Have you given them the opportunity to explore their own strengths and development areas?

■ What about using a profiling tool or psychometric assessment with them to identify what type of people they are – what preferences do they have?

■ What about the way that meetings are managed? Have you considered using an outside facilitator to help you establish how the team could meet more effectively?

One of the ways in which the facilitator could support the manager is by working with the team to create a team charter. If established early on it can save a lot of frustration for team participants. Essentially it means setting some behavioural guidelines. It is likely that the team members are equally frustrated about the way that team meetings are run and so involving them in setting standards around the team meetings will be an important way of achieving 'buy-in'.

A team charter could consist of the team undertaking to do the following:

- Turning up on time, staying until the end.

- Turning off mobile phones for the duration of the meeting, or at least setting to 'silent'.

- If essential calls have to be taken the participant leaves the room to take the call, returning promptly.

- Laptops ideally are not used, but if needed are only used for note taking, not for undertaking other work.

- People respect language/cultural differences, and allow everyone to contribute.

- People communicate through the chair and do not all talk at once, or over someone else.

- Meetings are managed efficiently and start and finish on time.

By creating a process or acceptable standards of behaviour some of the tensions can be removed from the meeting. As well as undertaking the activities with the team there is also the opportunity to work with the manager on a one-to-one basis. In the same way as the team may be profiled, the manager could also complete some kind of assessment using a psychometric or profiling tool. By doing this the personal coach has a starting point to understand more about the personal competencies of the manager.

Depending on the tool(s) used these assessments can help the manager gain insights about his individual team members' self esteem, the way that they react with others, their willingness to cope with and accept change and their desire to help others develop.

From this starting point the coach can help the manager begin to visualize how it could be different. Help learners to realize that if they believe things are not working they are in danger of reinforcing a negative. Encourage them instead to focus their energy and positive beliefs into making something work.

VISUALIZATION

Visualization is a very powerful tool in helping individuals to see alternatives, however initially some individuals will need a lot of support to realize its potential. Remember the saying 'If you keep on doing what you always did, you always get what you always got.' Personal coaching is about enabling people to see alternatives so that they don't always get what they always got. Achieving this shift in perspective will take time. Helping individuals to take small incremental steps towards another vision should ultimately lead to them beginning to have another view on the world (see Chapter 5).

CREATIVE PROBLEM SOLVING

For many people creative problem solving is about helping them to identify alternatives and offering support as they work through options. Often the issue or problem simply seems too big a challenge. Helping them to identify the issue and break it down into manageable chunks is an important first step. Then they can move forward using steps like these below.

1. Identify the problem.

2. Think around it.

3. Seek the involvement and views of interested people with differing views.

4. Isolate the problem and pay attention to it.

5. Use a variety of problem-solving techniques.

6. Think around the problem and explore all ideas and options.

7. Focus on solutions in a structured way.

8. Agree action plan for implementation.

9. Review and evaluate outcomes.

CREATING SPECIAL EVENTS

One of the positive activities that coaches can provide for their learners is to encourage them to create special learning events for themselves. The 'specialness' can vary enormously, but creating something memorable requires thinking outside the normal box of activities.

Most memorable learning experiences usually take place in a special environment. By recreating the sensation of that special event learners can apply the lessons learnt to different situations. This very much links to the concept of 'flow'. By remembering the sensation of special learning events it may be possible to enhance other learning situations.

By helping learners to recognize the value of doing things differently they will find learning and reflecting opportunities in a variety of different environments. Help them to recognize the importance of taking time out to think or reflect on what they have achieved or what they might want to do in the future.

One very valuable use of thinking is to encourage learners to reflect on their achievements or their learning, for example:

- Reviewing the past: what have I done and what have I learnt as a result of my experiences?

- The present: what do I need to think about? Why am I trying to find a solution?

- The future: what do I really want to do? What do I want to achieve?

- Setting stretch goals: if I really wanted to challenge myself, how would I take my ambition further?

Encourage them to use visualization to help them picture what it is they want to achieve. Help them to create a mental picture of what they want – to really try to see the images. Self-belief is a very powerful tool. When they find themselves in a situation that they are enjoying, suggest that they practise using their minds like a camera, really absorb the images, the colours – ask them to try to capture the scents and sounds. Encourage them to recapture this later. Your mind has the capacity to work for you, but it needs attention to achieve it.

WHEN IS IT THE RIGHT TIME TO SHARE THOUGHTS WITH OTHERS?

One of the interesting things about focusing on your learners' thinking is that they will become more aware of what they can achieve. This is particularly true if they think positive thoughts.

What is important is that the learner shares the right thoughts at the right time, because sometimes if we share our half-formed thoughts too soon other people can put a negative influence on us and dampen our enthusiasm. However we also often need a sounding board, someone we can trust with whom to share those embryonic ideas. As part of their support network, suggest that they identify people who can give them balanced feedback, who will help them to explore their hopes, dreams and aspirations.

One way of helping your learners to start using thinking time more effectively is to encourage them to use the following checklist:

■ What do I want to think about?

■ When is it the best time for me to think?

■ What can I do to help my thinking?

■ Who do I know that I can share my embryonic thoughts with?

■ How can I create the right environment in which to think?

■ Can I create a thinking zone, somewhere special where I can concentrate?

■ Who do I know who will stimulate my mind and help me to think?

It is important to help your learners recognize how their thought processes work and to remember to think about using their senses. The more they practise the more space they create for thinking and the richer will be the experience. They will come to cherish and value their thinking and reflecting time.

7

When the going gets tough

KNOWING WHEN TO GET HELP

It is important to recognize not only when you need to get help but where to get help.

One of the interesting challenges with personal coaching is recognizing the nature of the relationship and the support that you are offering. In today's working environment people react very differently to the pressures that they find themselves working under. Neither you nor the people that you are coaching can predict when you will find yourselves under additional pressure or having to work with exceptional circumstances.

If you have an ongoing personal coaching relationship then hopefully you will already have identified some ways to enable learners to work through difficult situations by adopting different types of coping strategy.

Sometimes, however, circumstances are such that the normal strategy that they usually adopt to cope isn't working. In these circumstances it is critically important that you act professionally, but also supportively.

DEVELOPING A COPING STRATEGY

A coping strategy is exactly as it is stated: it is a strategy for how to cope in difficult circumstances. A coping strategy should also include prevention as well as helping individuals to prepare for difficult situations that they may find themselves in. By being prepared, the potential impact of a difficult situation will be reduced.

It is important that your learners recognize that you are one of a number of skilled practitioners with whom they can work. Depending on the situation you may be able to support the learner while they work through the issue(s). However, it is very important to recognize when additional support should be offered. Within the context of personal coaching in a working environment, if your judgement is that someone needs additional support, help learners explore this option, but recognize that ultimately it is their decision.

Every situation will be different. Many organizations offer some kind of employee assistance scheme whereby an individual can be offered counselling support, but this is always confidential and is actioned by the individual. Where there is no support you might suggest that they consider counselling, or other support. It cannot be emphasized enough the importance of learners making up their own minds about doing this.

A coach should never take on the role of a counsellor unless professionally qualified in counselling and again the individual should recognize the significance of the difference. A coach can however continue to focus on the support necessary in the working environment, even if additional support is being offered. What should never happen is a personal coach suggesting that an individual needs additional specialist help and then abandoning the learner.

ACCESSING ENERGY

For many individuals, it may not be specialist help that is required, but instead they have a need to work things through and find alternative solutions. Helping learners recharge can be very valuable. One of the first ways of doing this is to help them recognize what energizes them and equally what drains them. We started to explore this in Chapters 1 and 2. What is important is that individual learners understand their bodies and their sources of energy. This may be related to their sleeping pattern, their nutrition and their energy patterns and things that they can do to access more energy. For many people it is often simply a need for regular exercise, a sensible balanced diet and the right amount of sleep. There are exceptions, however, and if there may be physiological reasons why learners are lacking in energy encourage them to see their GPs.

Much can be achieved by the establishment of regular patterns and as a coach you can help the individuals work through their lifestyle issues to achieve a more balanced lifestyle. In order to take this seriously they need to prepare, to create thinking time. It is also important to help them to try to clear some of the unwanted debris that may be cluttering up their minds. One useful action is to encourage your learners to think about how often in a working day they actually go outside to get fresh air.

As a starting point for relaxation encourage them to try to create space to think, to go somewhere quiet, and to just sit absolutely still, and to feel their heartbeats, becoming aware of sounds around them and feeling the tension drain away. Initially they may find it hard to clear their minds or to relax. For the first few times that they do this they should be under no pressure at all to do anything – encourage them to just sit still and enjoy the sensation of exploring their minds. Gradually they may find that they are able to begin to control their thoughts.

From this point help them to build in a plan of how they will regularly relax. Take time out for them. Begin to build a pattern where they feel more in control of their lives. This stage can take some time as individuals may have built up a complete pattern of living that they may initially find very hard to change. They may need help to try to make incremental changes, the techniques discussed in Chapters 2 and 5 can help with this.

DEALING WITH DIFFICULT PEOPLE

There may be occasions when your learners may find themselves in situations when they have to deal with people who are perceived as being difficult. As an initial step in developing a strategy for dealing with these situations help your learner to recognize that there are often two sides to every issue. However if there is a real difficulty encourage them to think about the person involved and to consider what they know about them, remind them about the model in Chapter 2. Suggest that they view the situation through the eyes of the other person. What is likely to be on that person's mind? What could be their issue? Help learners to explore how they might be feeling; suggest that they follow the strategy below and prepare carefully for any meetings:

- Think about what they know about the profile and the behaviour of the person they are meeting.

- Recognize their own profile and natural behaviours.

- In the meeting take time to assess the situation.

- Ask questions, listen to the other person's responses.

- Manage silence.

- Think through their own response.

- Work towards win-win outcomes.

- Work with them to find a solution.

- If action is agreed, follow it up.

- Learn from the experience.

- Be prepared for next time.

In your follow-up sessions with your learners encourage them to share how they felt. Would they do anything differently? What have they learnt?

USING FEEDBACK POSITIVELY

One way in which we really change our behaviour is through feedback from others. How open are your learners to feedback? Encourage them to actively seek the opinions of others who may have a different view-point. Do they ask for clarification and integrate the views of others with their perception of themselves? How prepared are they to accept the need to change? Once they have received feedback, how proactive are they in doing things differently? How willing are they to develop new ways of behaving?

Help them to develop an ability to go above their interaction with others and to recognize how effective they are being by reflecting on key conversations with others and ask themselves 'How effective was

I in that meeting?' Do they understand how their emotions affect their behaviour and the impact on others? This is one of the most sensitive areas of personal coaching. Your learners may perceive you as their 'friend' and that you are on 'their side' against what they may sometimes perceive as the rest of the world.

Gently helping them to explore that some of the issues may reside with them can be an invaluable but tough lesson. Help them to recognize the impact that they might have on others. Help them to recognize other people's body language, to read the signals, to treat people as individuals, to be sensitive, and to be prepared to modify their behaviour.

Encourage them to examine the ways that they give feedback to others and to observe their response. Do they agree, appreciate it, or feel that it is unjust? How do they know? What signals have they been given? Use the following checklist as a way of helping them to give feedback:

- Always start by asking the other person how they felt about the situation, or their performance.

- Then give their feedback starting with the positive.

- Build on their view, ask open questions to probe further, then make recommendations based on what they could do differently.

- Strive towards achieving win-win outcomes, be objective, seek clarification on behaviour.

- Agree next stage actions.

- Finish positively.

Always follow through on feedback – tell people what you have achieved or attempted to do differently as a result of their feedback. Remember there is a right place and a right time for giving feedback. Respect an individual's right to privacy for these conversations. Help the learner to recognize that giving feedback is a development area for many people, and the better that they get to know themselves, the better able they will be able to help others to give them effective feedback. Also point out that not all feedback may be appropriate, or accurate. Encourage learners to seek additional help by asking others for their viewpoint.

COPING WITH AMBIGUITY

We have already established several times that everyone is different. For some people ambiguity is very threatening: they want certainty in their lives and ambiguous situations cause them difficulties. In these circumstances a coach can help them to explore the reasons for their discomfort and help them cope more effectively in the future.

To help them cope more readily it is important to establish with them what helps or hinders the situation. Encourage them to think about previous ambiguous situations, ask them:

- 'What made the situation ambiguous?'
- 'How did you handle the situation?'
- 'What was the outcome?'
- 'What did you learn?'

Then encourage them to think about a current situation, use open questions such as:

- 'What aspects cause you the most difficulty?'
- 'What do you really know about this situation?'

- 'Why is it important to anchor down information?'
- 'How do you feel when situations are unclear?'
- 'What could your manager/colleagues do to help?'
- 'What could you do to help yourself?'

Using their responses to these questions help your learners work through the reasons why they are uncomfortable with ambiguity and to develop a strategy for coping in the future. Help them to understand the importance of not jumping to conclusions and not believing rumours but instead asking for information appropriately. Do they really show respect for others, or do they override the objections or feelings of others in their anxiety to sort out an issue? It is most important to help them to develop self-belief, and a strategy for coping with those occasions when they simply may have to wait for information.

OVERCOMING OBSTACLES

One of the main reasons why someone may elicit the help of a personal coach is to help them overcome obstacles. The obstacles may be associated with an interaction with an individual, or a situation but, on their own, learners may find it difficult to resolve the situation and to overcome potential obstacles. Suggest that they take time to listen to the views of others, formulate their opinions and reply positively. Encourage them to position their viewpoint with tact and diplomacy.

A personal coach can be a valuable sounding board in enabling the individual to work through a situation and to identify ways in which they could do things differently. Again the coach can help learners work through the situation logically asking them to identify:

- the nature of the situation;
- the details of the obstacle;

- the frequency of it occurring;
- what they have done to date to resolve it;
- what has worked;
- what has been less successful.

By working through step-by-step and highlighting the issues you can support learners as they identify where the issues lie and how to create a strategy for the future. Always encourage them to look for support from their manager or colleagues. Encourage them to answer the following:

- 'How resilient am I?'
- 'How willing am I to accept feedback and really respond positively to it?'
- 'Do I have a strong sense of my own self-worth and capabilities?'
- 'How carefully do I prepare before giving feedback to others or do I just want to get rid of it quickly via e-mail or a quick conversation?'

Help them to be aware that they do not necessarily have to accept the status quo. It is appropriate, however, to help them to recognize when it is time to walk away from a situation. However high their resolve, however committed they are to finding a solution, there will be times when the best solution really is to walk away. Sometimes by doing that the situation changes to one that can be more easily resolved. Often by talking it through learners will identify their own solutions. As with most things the solution often lies with the learners, but they have to own it and want to change.

Equally for each obstacle there may be many solutions. The secret is to find the right one. One valuable activity that a personal coach can undertake with learners is to work through a number of situations and help the learners identify what they would do if that situation arose in reality. By preparing for them and working out a strategy it will be less daunting if the situations actually occur.

As mentioned in the other chapters it is important, when supporting learners who are working through difficult situations, that you help them to relax, recharge and celebrate the incremental successes along the way. This is particularly relevant when working with behavioural issues. Use inspirational quotations, pictures, and sometimes arrange to meet in more relaxed surroundings to help them step outside some of the more challenging situations that they may find themselves in.

8

Creating your own support network

The reality of working as a personal coach is that there will be times when you need to recharge and create your own space to reignite your own energy levels. It is very easy to keep going and to ignore warning signals.

People who help others are often not very good at looking after themselves. One way to overcome this is to create your own support network. Within this network it is important to identify people who will provide you with different kinds of support. Do you have a network of people who can stimulate, energize and support you?

If you are offering one-to-one support to a number of people it is essential that you adopt a policy of looking after yourself, knowing your preferences and style of working, understanding your energy levels, and building in regular short breaks. These are all essential to your overall well-being. You need to build a portfolio of strategies to help you relax and take care of yourself. Finding ways of centring and calming are essential, particularly if you travel and stay away in different locations. It is really important to maintain your pattern and routine around bedtime, food, exercise so that your life will be less disrupted. Some people find that yoga, relaxation or breathing exercises can help you to learn a discipline of switching off, which in turn can lead to improved sleeping patterns. You might also want to explore homeopathic or alternative remedies, but always consult your own GP or alternative remedy practitioner because there can be a danger in creating your own cocktail of remedies.

As you progress through your career you learn more and more about your physical and mental states, but to take effective care of yourself requires discipline. It is so easy to push yourself that little bit harder, to do just one more piece of work, and because you are responding to your client's or participant's needs you keep going when perhaps you should be taking a break. The long-term solution is to look after your body and mind in the same way that someone would maintain a cherished piece of machinery.

Protecting thinking time is even harder, particularly when other people have access to your diaries. In offices with electronic networking it becomes even more important to protect your time. Very few people actually enter into their diaries 'thinking time' because of their fear of the comments that such an entry might generate. Many open-plan offices limit the opportunity to think creatively and people often find it difficult to say assertively 'I need space and quiet to think.' However, increasingly organizations are recognizing the importance of innovation and creativity and are encouraging a more positive approach to an individual's need for space and thinking time. Personal coaching may not appear to need the same level of preparation as a training course but, in fact, the preparation and follow up are essential to ensure that you have come to the session focused on the needs of your learner and that you are mentally alert enough to undertake the coaching process effectively and to react to the varying needs of your learner throughout the session. The levels of concentration in a one-to-one session are incredibly high and both you and your learner will need to recognize the impact that these sessions will have and build in a 'cool down' at the end of the session to allow both of you to record and reflect on what has been achieved.

PREVENTING BURNOUT

Creative, artistic and busy professional people are potentially susceptible to 'burnout'. Prevention is better than cure and all the measures mentioned below are relevant. With experience you will be better able to manage your life pressures to achieve a balance. There are specific actions that you can take to minimize the risk. This list may also be relevant to your learner:

■ Get to know yourself. Find out how much sleep you need on a regular basis and try to achieve at least an average number of hours sleep per week.

■ Eat properly. Find a diet that gives you the proper balance of foods for your lifestyle.

■ Take some form of exercise. Choose something that you can do regularly and that gives you an opportunity to meet other people.

■ Develop a network of professional colleagues and friends that you can use to support you. Particularly important are people who motivate and inspire you or who make you laugh – humour is a great stress reliever.

■ Regularly undertake professional development: identify new skills or areas of expertise.

■ Each day create space, however little, just for yourself. Whatever other work or domestic pressures exist, devote some time to yourself. Use it to do something relaxing – read a book, listen to music, telephone someone, clear something out of your personal action list, or just stare into space.

■ Recognize your achievement. It is wonderful when other people give you positive feedback but reviewing your own progress can equally be positive, particularly if you have logged your starting point.

■ Be alert to the signals of too much pressure and do something before you reach the symptoms of stress.

■ Build variety into your working life. Try not to fall into the routine of 'I'm coaching Bill therefore it must be Thursday.'

■ Set yourself lifetime goals and regularly review progress against them.

Lifetime ambitions can only be achieved from a position of personal strength. One of the oldest books about self-motivation is *Think and Grow Rich* by Napoleon Hill. This book and many others illustrate the importance of taking control, rather than letting other people, situations, or circumstances control *you*. Whatever personal goal you are trying to achieve, it is important that you stop and regularly reconfirm to yourself 'I can do it!' This illustrates the power of faith and of self-belief and, as Hill says, 'Directed faith makes every thought crackle with power. You can rise to limitless heights, impelled by the lifting force of your mighty new self-confidence.'

SELF-KNOWLEDGE

How well do you know yourself?

- Can you accurately describe your strengths and areas of development?

- Do you really understand how you will react in different circumstances?

- Do you listen to advice from other people?

- Have you received feedback that has helped you to gain insight into your personality or the way you react to others?

- Are you someone that others turn to? Do you inspire trust? Do you help others through the tough times? Giving an impression of quiet confidence can inspire others.

- What could you do to be more consistent in your support?

- How aware are you of your communication style? Would others describe you as an effective communicator?

- How easy do you find it to switch off? How often do you take time to socialize with others informally both in and out of work?

- Do you seek to broaden your perspective by taking time to mix with people with different interests, backgrounds, people who may challenge you?

The more insight you gain the better able you are to self-motivate and to harness your energy and talents to achieve your dreams. Many hopes and dreams never come to fruition because people make it too difficult for themselves to achieve them. The greater your self knowledge the more able you are to create the situations and to identify the support that will help you to help others.

LOOK IN THE MIRROR

One of the most important actions that you can do is to get to know yourself and how you react in different situations. Add to this picture by talking to others, listen to what they say, build up a picture of your skills and qualities, explore your personality traits and take as much feedback as possible. Look in the mirror. What do you see?

Ultimately it is your picture of yourself that you are building and only by exposing yourself to different situations and people will you add richness to your understanding of yourself. We need to know how to get the best from others and how to give the best of ourselves.

We need to understand why we get on well with some people and to find ways of working and respecting other people with whom we may have less natural affinity. Much of this is to do with our perspective on the world, but also our work and lifestyle preferences. The more you understand the reasons behind your natural preferences the more able you will be to progress on your personal journey.

TAKE TIME TO TALK

Who do you talk to? By this I do not mean gossip or idle chit-chat, but really talking in a way that actually means something. The sale of mobile phones increases every day. All the telecommunications companies are competing for your air time and yet if you analysed the time you spend on the phone and the size of your phone bill and asked yourself if it really made you, or the person on the other end of the line, feel better you may find a surprising result. This is particularly true of mobile phones. You are more likely to come off the phone completely frustrated and exhausted at being cut off every time you lose a signal.

Contrast that with the feeling you experience when you sit down and talk with someone you care for, or someone who has really listened to you, given you valuable advice, or simply made you laugh. We are constantly reading about the increase of pressure, the loss of free time, or couples who are too tired to make a decision about which takeaway to order, or who make deals with each other about who will put out the dustbin or do the shopping.

Conversations that start with 'We need to talk' strike fear into either partner as it is seen as the preamble to some kind of relationship breakdown.

Unfortunately as we get older we realize with regret that perhaps we did not talk to our children enough or perhaps tell our partners or parents how much we love them. We are all too busy. Weeks go by and we forget to call, the letter we meant to write never gets written. We are told that the art of conversation is dead. In the age of the e-mail we converse in broken sentences, blunt and to the point, and yet even e-mail can be used to link families across the globe, to allow children to communicate with parents, to allow business people to talk to their families.

Talking to people by whatever means is vitally important, it is a lifeline that can stimulate your mind, bring happiness and security, knowing that you have people who care. With dramatic changes in people's work or lifestyles they are often encouraged to talk to people in their network. It is then that you may realize that you have far fewer people to talk to than you thought. It is better to start growing your network now than wait until a crisis triggers it.

GET UNDER YOUR SKIN

If you believe in yourself it is much easier to convince others to believe in you. Self-belief comes from within. Others can reinforce it, but first you need to plant the seed. Every national sports team develops confidence by encouraging team members to understand their individual strengths. The team coach works to build personal strength, team cohesion and belief in the team's ability to win. If you are really going to help others achieve their personal learning goals you need to believe in your own ability – you need to develop an inner resilience to help you keep going through difficult times.

There is a strong belief by the writers of many personal development and self-help books that if you really believe in something you can make it happen. It is the power of positive thought. Another way of describing it is 'self-talk'. Shad Helmstetter (1998) in *What to Say When You Talk to Yourself* argues powerfully about the need to programme your brain into positive thoughts rather than the negative messages that we receive in our lives (see Chapter 2).

In your work as a personal coach you may be working with learners who have had their self-confidence regularly knocked by others. If you believe in the power of positive thought you are more likely to be able to help others develop their own self-belief.

You may also want to pursue a particular goal or ambition yourself. If so, some of the activities in Chapter 2 may also be appropriate for you to consider, but as a starting point you may like to review the following questions:

- What is my personal vision?

- What would I like to do next?

- What are my SMART objectives?

- Who do I know who can help me?

- What are the key actions that will help me?

- What might stop me?

- How can I reinforce the activities that will help me?

- How can I overcome what might stop me?

- What is the first thing that I am going to do to get started?

- How will I know that I have been successful?

And after you have achieved your own personal goal:

- Recognize your achievement.

- Review it against your objectives and action plan.

- Make sure you capture all your memories and successes and what you have learned about how you prefer to learn.

- Talk to your own coach, and your network. Let them know what you have achieved. Thank them for their support.

- Plan what you want to do next.

- Start the same process of setting goals and outlining your next SMART objectives.

- Celebrate what you have achieved!

Finally, recognize what a special role you are developing as a personal coach: the self-belief, the ability to listen to others, the care and compassion is not just relevant in your work. Use it to develop and share in your relationships with others, your friends, your partner, your parents and children.

Bibliography

Belasco, J (1990) *Teaching the Elephant to Dance: Empowering change in your organisation*, Hutchinson Business, London

Belbin, M (1981) *Management Teams*, Heinemann, London

Black, J (1994) *Mindstore*, Thorsons, London

Bohm, D and Lee, N (1996) *On Dialogue*, Routledge, London

Brown, M (1993) *The Dinosaur Strain*, Innovation Centre Europe Ltd, Polegate, East Sussex

Buzan, T (1995) *Use Your Head*, BBC, London

Buzan, T and Buzan, B (1993) *The Mind Map Book*, BBC, London

Csikzentmihalyi, M (1990) *Flow*, Harper & Row, London

Gardner, H (1993) *Frames of Mind*, Basic Books, New York

Gawain, Shakti (1995) *Creative Visualization*, New World Library, Novato CA

Goleman, D (1999) *Working with Emotional Intelligence*, Bloomsbury, London

Grigg, J (1997) *Portfolio Working: A practical guide to thriving in a changing workplace*, Kogan Page, London

Grinder, J and Bandler, R, *Frogs into Princes: Neuro-linguistic programming*

Hammer, M and Champy, J (1993) *Re-engineering the Corporation*, HarperCollins, New York and Nicholas Brealey, London

Handy, C (1994) *The Empty Raincoat*, Hutchinson, London

Handy, C (1995) *Beyond Certainty*, Hutchinson, London

Heller, R (1998) *In Search of European Excellence*, HarperCollins Business, London

Helmstetter, S (1998) *What to Say When You Talk to Yourself*, Cynus

Hill, N (1990) *Think and Grow Rich*, Fawcett Books

Jaworski, J and Senge, P (1998) *Synchronicity*, Berrett-Koeler, San Francisco

Kanter, R (1983) *The Change Masters*, Allen & Unwin, London

Kanter, R (1989) *When Giants Learn to Dance*, Simon & Schuster, London

Kolb, D, Rubin, I and McIntyre, J (1994) *Organisational Psychology: An experiential approach to organisational behavior*, Prentice-Hall, London

Malone, S (1997) *How to Set Up and Manage a Corporate Learning Centre*, Gower, Aldershot

McNally, David (1993) *Even Eagles Need a Push*, Thorsons, London

O'Connor, J and Seymour, J (1990) *Introducing NLP*, Mandala, London

O'Connor, J and Seymour, J (1994) *Training with NLP: Skills for managers, trainers and communicators*, Thorsons, London

Peters, T (1992) *Liberation Management*, Macmillan, London

Peters, T (1997) *The Circle of Innovation*, Hodder & Stoughton, London

Peters, T and Austin, N (1985) *A Passion for Excellence*, Collins, London

Redfield, J (1998) *The Celestine Vision*, Bantam Books, London

Salovey, P, Mayer, J D and Caruso, D R (1997) *Emotional Intelligence Meets Traditional Standards for an Intelligence*, unpublished manuscript

Scott, A (1997) *Learning Centres: A step-by-step guide to planning, managing and evaluating an organizational resource centre*, Kogan Page, London

Semler, R (1993) *Maverick*, Arrow, London

Senge, P (1990) *The Fifth Discipline*, Doubleday, New York

Slater, R (1998) *Jack Welch and the GE Way: Management insights and leadership secrets of the legendary CEO*, McGraw-Hill, Maidenhead

Thorne, K (1998) *Training Places, Choosing and Using Venues for Training*, Kogan Page, London

Thorne, K and Machray, A (1998) *Training on a Shoestring*, Kogan Page, London

Thorne, K and Machray, A (2000) *World Class Training — Providing training excellence*, Kogan Page, London

Bibliography

Thorne, K and Mackey, D (2001) *Everything You Ever Needed to Know About Training*, Kogan Page, London

Whitmore, J (1996) *Coaching for Performance*, Nicholas Brealey, London

By the same author

Everything You Ever Needed to Know About Training: A complete step-by-step guide to training and development (2001) 2nd edn, Kogan Page, London (co-authored with David Mackey)

Training on a Shoestring: Getting the most from your time, your budgets and your staff (1998) Kogan Page, London (co-authored with Alex Machray)

Training Places: Choosing and using venues for training (1998) Kogan Page, London

World Class Training: Providing training excellence (2000) Kogan Page, London (co-authored with Alex Machray)

Index